CAIRO PAPERS
VOLUME 34

MW01295216

Organizing
the Unorganized
Migrant Domestic Workers in Lebanon

Farah Kobaissy

THE AMERICAN UNIVERSITY IN CAIRO PRESS
CAIRO   NEW YORK

Cover photo: Migrant Workers Parade by Pat Sy

This paperback edition first published in 2023 by
The American University in Cairo Press
113 Sharia Kasr el Aini, Cairo, Egypt
420 Lexington Avenue, Suite 1644, New York, NY 10170
www.aucpress.com

First published in an electronic edition in 2016

ISBN 978 1 649 03233 1

Names: Kobaissy, Farah, author.
Title: Organizing the unorganized : migrant domestic workers in Lebanon /
    Farah Kobaissy.
Identifiers: LCCN 2022016016 | ISBN 9781649032331 (paperback) | ISBN
    9781617978531 (epub) | ISBN 9781617977329 (adobe pdf)
Subjects: LCSH: Women household employees--Lebanon. | Women household
    employees--Labor unions--Lebanon. | Women migrant labor--Lebanon. |
    Labor unions--Lebanon.
Classification: LCC HD6072.2.L3 K63 2022 | DDC
    331.4/810095692--dc23/eng/20220504

1 2 3 4 5   27 26 25 24 23

Designed by Adam el-Sehemy

Contents

تنظيم العمالة غير المنظمة
عاملات المنازل الوافدات في لبنان

فرح قبيسي

في ٤ مايو ٢٠١٥، تزامنا مع يوم العمال العالمي، خرج المئات من عاملات المنازل الوافدات ومؤيديهن الى الشارع مطالبين الحكومة اللبنانية بالاعتراف القانوني بنقابتهن.

وكان وزير العمل اللبناني قد استنكر خطوة إنشاء النقابة بوصفها عملا غير قانوني من شأنه أن يخلق مزيدا من المشكلات بدلا من حلها.

هذا الموقف يعكس مخاوف الدولة من قيام تنظيمات عمالية، خاصة من قبل العمالة الأجنبية، تخرج هذه الطبقة من اطارها المهمش وتحفر لها مكانا في الفضاء السياسي والاجتماعي العام.

يقوم هذا البحث بإلقاء الضوء على هذه التجربة من خلال دراسة عملية تشكيل كيان نقابي لعاملات المنازل الأجنبيات في لبنان بالتعاون مع الاتحاد الوطني لنقابات العمال والمستخدمين ومنظمة العمل الدولية وبعض منظمات المجتمع المدني المهتمة بحقوق الانسان وحقوق المرأة والوقوف عند أهم التحديات التي تواجه هذا المشروع. وفي هذا الإطار، تتعرض الدراسة للنضال الجماعي لعاملات المنازل لتحسين وضعهن الاقتصادي والاجتماعي من خلال التنظيم النقابي الذي يسعين لتكوينه والطرق التي يلجأن اليها لإكساب المهنة الاحترام اللائق بها عن طريق إعادة تعريف ماهية وظروف العمل الذي يقمن به. وهنا تتناول الباحثة علاقات القوة المتعددة التي تساهم في تشكيل هذه النقابة والتي تتمحور حول إنتماءات الطبقة والنوع والعرق والجنسية. كما أنها تضع هذه المحاولة في الإطار الأشمل لنضال الحركة العمالية في ظل النظام النيوليبرالي وحركة حقوق المرأة.

Acknowledgments

I have incurred endless debts to many people who supported me throughout the journey of completing this study. I owe this work primarily to the members of the executive board of the trade union for domestic workers in Lebanon, who provided the context for the research. I can never be grateful enough for their generosity with their time and resources. I am deeply grateful to Mala, Lily, Gemma, Rose, Suzanne, and Maryam, whose courage and steadfastness inspired me to write and to finish the thesis upon which this work is based.

I am also deeply indebted to Martina Rieker, my academic supervisor, and to Hanan Sabea and Ray Jureidini, the readers of my research, for their continued guidance and insightful comments on the evolving forms of the thesis. Martina's tireless academic, political, and personal commitment toward her students, her unwavering support for us, her endless teasing and sense of humor, constituted part and parcel of my journey and made the MA years a time of true learning and maturing. Many people in the academy have also guided me through the journey of formulating this research and preparing for it. Their own work and their engagement with my research is affirming. I would like to thank Jennifer Yvette Terrel, Arunima Gopinath, and Mallarika Sinha Roy.

This research would not have been completed without the nurturing group of friends and colleagues at the Center for Gender and Women's Studies at the American University in Cairo, who read earlier drafts of the thesis and shared their ideas and academic critiques throughout the writing phase. I owe the many hours of writing, crying, laughing, and support to Kenza Youssefi, Menna Mourad, Sabrina Lilleby, and Sara Verderi.

The research would also not have been possible without the support of friends and family. Special thanks are owed to Maya Elhelou and Mostafa Mohie, whose continuous encouragement, comments, and discussions inspired many of the ideas presented here, as well as to Nabil Abdo, Nidal Ayoub, Hisham Ashkar, Ghassan Makarem, Farah Salka, and Nadine Moawad, whose love, activism, and untiring commitment to social change were and will always be a source of inspiration. I also thank Nadine, Ghassan, and Hisham for helping editing parts of the thesis. To Aslam Khan, who tried his best, despite the distance, to continuously feed my soul with much-needed love. And finally to my mother Olfat and my father "Haidarof," who have always provided encouragement for my education and choices in life, however awkward they seemed. This monograph is dedicated to their labor.

CHAPTER 1

Beyond the Weapons of the Weak: Domestic Workers' Union in Lebanon

We are here today celebrating equality for all.
Migrants and nationals join together as one.
So, domestic workers, stop dying.
It's time to rejoice and strive . . .
Heal Beirut,
Make it a better place
For you and me
And the entire workers' race.
There are migrants dying.
Do you care for their living?
Make it a better place
For you and for me.

(Extract from a song written and sung
by the domestic workers' unionists during the
launching of their union on January 25, 2015.)

On Sunday, May 4, 2015, the occasion of International Workers' Day, hundreds of migrant domestic workers and their allies in Lebanon took to the streets, demanding that their union be formally recognized by the Lebanese government. The union has been denounced by the labor minister as "illegal," arguing that it will only "generate problems" instead of solving them. The minister suggested that "protection" for domestic workers is best guaranteed through "new laws," not through union organizing.[1] In other words, rights are unequivocally the government's grant, not to be claimed or bargained for. He added: "Protection takes place through procedures, not through the introduction of the domestic workers into political and class games."[2] The minister's last statement blatantly expresses the state of fear generated by the thought of workers organizing, migrants in particular, who through their attempt are putting a foot out of their 'zone of exception' into the political and the social space of the nation.

Various sources estimate the number of migrant domestic workers in Lebanon between 150,000 and 200,000 in an overall work force of 1.45 million (Tayah 2012:9). In a country where state provisions for childcare and care for the elderly are absent, the burden falls on the nuclear family, and women in particular, to cope with the organization of care and domestic work. Cheap and precarious migrant domestic labor represents a low-cost solution to the Lebanese care deficit. It is estimated that one in every four families in Lebanon employs a migrant domestic worker (Jureidini 2011a).

As the number of migrant domestic workers gradually grew in the 1990s, along with the increase of reported cases of abuse in the 2000s, civil-society groups began to take initiatives to highlight and address these violations. Women's-rights and human-rights organizations (both local and international) came to supplement church-led charity organizations that had been working since the 1980s on offering safe spaces for migrants, including domestic workers, offering charity, communal ceremonies, prayers, and legal and social assistance (Moors et al. 2009). Tayah (2012) distinguishes two time periods for these interventions: the first is the era dominated by churches and faith-based associations (1980–2005); the second is the period following the 2006 establishment of the National Steering Committee on Migrant Domestic Workers (which includes the International Labour Organization [ILO], human-rights organizations, the Placement Agencies' Syndicate, and the Ministry of Labor). The actions of non-governmental organizations (NGOs) on behalf of the migrant domestic workers sometimes intersect with the actions of faith-based organizations. However, the period

---

1   "Mou'tamar ta'sisi li naqabet 'amelat wa o'mal al-manazel: khotwa oula li-l-difa' 'an al-huquq," *Naharnet*, January 25, 2015.

2   "Sejel wazir al-'amal Sejaan Azzi," *al-Akhbar*, May 8, 2015.

since 2006 has seen a more substantive role for NGOs and brought new dimensions to the struggle for domestic workers' rights. However, the primary approach remained dominated by humanitarian focus on cases of violence, trafficking, and deaths at the expense of labor rights. As a result, "migrant domestic workers are first and foremost portrayed as victims duped by agents and exploited and mistreated by employers" (Moors et al. 2009). This dominant approach, besides emphasizing the plight of domestic workers, failed to address the unequal power relations between workers and employers. Kerbage (2014) argues that throughout the second era, workers remained to a large extent excluded from expressing their demands and addressing the authorities in their own name without intermediaries. Workers were also excluded from negotiations with state authorities, embassies, and recruitment and placement agencies. Despite the fact that the work of these NGOs succeeded in pressuring the Lebanese state to take action on small areas of reform, such as the unified standard contract in 2009[3] and the draft law for domestic workers in 2011,[4] these measures preserved the *kafala* (sponsorship) system and further institutionalized the exclusion of domestic workers from normal labor interactions (Esim and Kerbage 2011).

Motaparthy (2015) defines the *kafala* as a "system of control" and as a way for governments to delegate responsibility for migrants to private citizens or companies. She argues that the system gives sponsors a set of legal abilities to control workers:

Without the employer's permission, workers cannot change jobs, quit jobs, or leave the country. If a worker leaves a job without permission, the employer has the power to cancel his or her residence visa, automatically turning the worker into an illegal resident in the country.

---

3 The unified standard contract is a model contract with which the employer of migrant workers needs to comply before work permits are issued by the Ministry of Labor. It stipulates a minimum of rights for migrant domestic workers, such as the right to adequate food and clothing. Other terms of the contract include guarantees of a weekly day of rest and annual holidays. It limits the number of working hours per day to ten. It gives the workers the right to quit their workplace if they are abused, and it obliges the employers to arrange health insurance for the workers.

4 In February 2011, labor minister Boutros Harb proposed a draft law to regulate the work of migrant domestic workers that would keep the current *kafala* system in place, but his draft law was abandoned when a change in government took place.

Workers whose employers cancel their residency visas often have to leave the country through deportation proceedings, and many have to spend time behind bars. (Motaparthy 2015)

Their fragile condition is further exacerbated by the discrimination they face as poor migrant women who work in a profession that lacks social and formal recognition.

The noticeable distinction that has emerged over the last decade is that the needs and interests of migrant domestic workers in Lebanon have overwhelmingly been the concern of NGOs rather than trade unions. Recently, this started to shift when the National Federation of Workers and Employees' Trade Unions in Lebanon (FENASOL) began to organize domestic workers, who are predominantly migrants with few Lebanese nationals, marking the third era in the struggle for domestic workers' rights. Yet this new era is far from disentangling itself from the previous one. On the contrary, the trade union for domestic workers was formed based on cooperation among FENASOL, the ILO, Kafa (Enough Violence, a women's-rights organization), Insan (a human-rights organization), and the Migrant Community Center (MCC, a center run by the Anti-Racism Movement in Beirut).

Contextualizing the Domestic Workers' Union

The year 2015 marked a shift in the history of organizing migrant workers in Lebanon. It witnessed the birth of the first trade union for domestic workers under the umbrella of FENASOL. The Federation's initiative to organize domestic workers was supported by the ILO. A report published by the ILO in 2012 recommended that

NGOs are expected to engage workers' unions in the planning and implementation of relevant programs and activities if only to emphasize the 'worker' in domestic workers. When unions become thoroughly informed about the working and living conditions of domestic workers, their commitment to domestic workers' issues during tripartite dialogues on migrant workers becomes more significant. (Tayah 2012:56)

In fact, the ILO global agenda on domestic workers, following the adoption of the ILO Convention 189 in 2011 on domestic work, emphasized the need for local trade-union federations to act as partners to organize domestic workers and ultimately push toward a tripartite negotiation among the state, workers, and employers/placement agencies. This coincided with local dynamics among trade unions in Lebanon as well as regional uprisings, all of which have played a role to the benefit of domestic workers.

In 2012, FENASOL, which is tied to the Lebanese Communist Party (LCP), made the decision to withdraw its membership from the General Confederation of Lebanese Workers (CGTL), the sole official representative of workers on the state level. The CGTL suffers from an ineffective bureaucracy, as well as extremely poor membership and participation on the part of the workers, as will be discussed in chapter 2. Following this move, FENASOL, which itself was not free from structural problems similar to the CGTL, needed and wanted to assert itself as an alternative model to the latter and compete over the status of workers' representation in Lebanon. The withdrawal came as a reaction to CGTL's leadership alliance with the employers, conceding to a minimum wage less than that proposed by the former minister of labor, Charbel Nahas, and refusing to allow the universal health coverage proposed by Nahas to be financed from taxing real-estate profits and financial speculation. The CGTL notoriously made history in demanding a minimum wage scale less than what a labor minister had proposed. FENASOL's withdrawal was criticized by many labor activists and journalists as too little, too late;[5] it was felt that its leadership, together with the leadership of the Communist Party, should have made this decision years earlier in order to stop the continuous process of weakening that the trade-union movement in Lebanon had been suffering since the 1990s. The LCP leadership justified this delay based on the belief that they could have a stronger say within the CGTL. Also, both leaderships (LCP and FENASOL) long defended the unity of the trade-union movement even when the trade union lost its representation of workers, and even when this unity meant uniting with the leadership of the CGTL, which has betrayed workers' interests on many occasions. However, in 2012, FENASOL finally found it was impossible to continue with this 'unholy marriage' with the Confederation.

---

5 M. Zbeeb, "A Nation Living Day to Day," *al-Akhbar English*, May 31, 2012, http://english.al-akhbar.com/node/7917.

The decision to withdraw also came within a national context of intensified labor mobilization within the informal, formal, public, and private sectors. Spinneys (a supermarket chain) workers were fighting a unionization battle, while contract workers of the Lebanese Electric Company, Hariri hospitals, Lebanese University, and Casino du Liban were on strike for fixed employment. Teachers in private and public schools, along with public employees, were fighting a long battle for wage increases, with strikes and protests reaching the tens of thousands. The common denominator among these labor struggles, beside the common experience of precarity, was their lack of formal union organization, which made their actions weak and unable to fully obtain their demands. Hence CGTL's inefficiency and betrayal of workers, as well as the intensification of labor protests, reopened the public discussion on the need for a democratic, independent, and representative labor movement in Lebanon. But this discussion was not only local; it was also taking place at the regional level within the revolutionary context of 2011 in the Arab world. Workers formed independent trade-union federations as alternatives to the state-led federations in Egypt and Yemen, and union organizing played a leading role in the popular uprisings against dictatorships in Tunisia and Bahrain.

In response to these local and regional developments, the CGTL issued a statement on December 20, 2012 accusing anyone who wants to establish an independent trade union of seeking to atomize, dismember, and divide the trade unions and abandon the workers in order to serve the "Zionist project" calling for constructive chaos. The ILO had been working to assist the formation of independent trade-union federations or support the ones that already existed. The case of Lebanon was in the middle, in the sense that there was no real independent trade-union federation but the FENASOL leadership was willing to form one, particularly if this meant technical and financial support from the ILO and other international trade-union organizations. In light of their accusation of being at the service of the Zionists, ILO officials became more determined to support and work with FENASOL as an exclusive partner in Lebanon. As a result, FENASOL decided on three main priorities:

1. To pressure the Lebanese parliament into adopting the 1948 ILO Convention no. 87 on freedom of association and protection of the

right to organize. This move was envisaged to liberate union action from administrative control of the Ministry of Labor and to allow public employees to create their own trade unions. Under the current Lebanese law, public employees are prevented from forming and joining trade unions, and from striking or taking any kind of collective action.

2. To change the internal structure of FENASOL into a democratic and inclusive organization of workers from all nationalities.
3. To organize informal workers.

Interestingly, the FENASOL leadership focused on organizing migrant domestic workers, while other informal-sector workers continue to be sidelined from the Federation outreach and organizational agenda. This difference will be discussed further in chapter 4.

Thus, within the context of local, regional, and global events and the intersection of opposing and colluding agendas of national and international actors, the trade union for domestic workers was established on January 25, 2015. The unionization of domestic workers brought focus to the labor dimension of migrant domestic workers' experiences, which had previously been sidelined in academic and activist discourse that had framed domestic workers primarily as victims of "modern-day slavery."

Beyond the Weapons of the Weak

In a recent discussion with my mother about my research on domestic workers in Lebanon, she said, "These workers are treated like slaves, in the full sense of the word." To support her argument, she added: "Go to Google and you will see pictures of them being abused. You will read stories of them being denied food, denied rest and vacations, overworked, sexually harassed, and killed." My working mother is not an activist and has never employed a live-in domestic worker; her knowledge about the plight of domestic workers in the country was mainly drawn from media reports, television shows, and newspaper articles that have proliferated in the last few years, highlighting cases of abused domestic workers. This coverage gave her a critical lens about the ways in which some of our relatives treated their live-in domestic workers, a treatment that she described as amounting to "racism."

The media's growing interest in the subject was the consequence of the work undertaken by NGOs. However, the focus of these NGOs on women migrant domestic workers in isolation from other kinds of migrant workers, and from workers in general, framed the domestic workers as an exceptional category, whose working experiences differ from those of other members of the working class. The overworked body of a Syrian construction worker, for instance, does not receive the same attention that the migrant domestic worker's abused body receives. And while the *kafala* system for migrant domestic workers is highlighted on the grounds that it allows the abuse of the worker by the employer, the same system as it applies to other migrant workers, binding them to their employers in the same way, does not get the same attention. When earlier in 2015 the minister of labor issued a decree extending the *kafala* system to the Syrian workers in Lebanon, who were previously exempted from the sponsorship requirement, none of the NGOs opposing the *kafala* system for migrant domestic workers protested, nor did FENASOL. One of the responses I received regarding this silence is that the Syrian workers in Lebanon constitute a "political issue" rather than a "purely" labor issue. Hence, for the NGOs it is safe to speak about domestic workers' exploitation within the familiar depoliticized human-rights framework since it avoids the 'dirty' field of politics. Thus, boundaries are being drawn between the labor issues and the political as separate spheres.

Going back to my discussion with my mother, she was very reluctant to follow my proposition to look at the shared experience of labor exploitation of the domestic workers and other workers. She said, "It's the responsibility of the trade unions to speak up on behalf of the Syrian workers. It's not the responsibility of the NGOs." When I asked for further clarification regarding this 'division of labor' between the trade unions and the NGOs, she added: "The domestic workers are disrespected and abused. This is why the NGOs should talk about them." In differentiating between the role of the NGOs and the role of the trade unions, she made a distinction between the people she considers as 'workers' who should be defended by labor unions, on the one side, and on the other side, the 'victims of abuse' who should be defended by NGOs. In other words, the domestic workers are not considered workers; they are recognized only in their identity as abused women.

This framework is similar to the one being employed by many NGOs working for the rights of domestic workers. And this, I argue, deepens the state of exception of domestic workers, when the discourse only concentrates on incidents of extreme abuse and addresses the state to "decrease the vulnerability of the migrant domestic workers" (Hamill 2011:6), rather than pushing for the full guarantee of the migrant domestic workers' labor rights. The discourse on extreme victimhood and slavery-like working conditions of domestic workers has also been the angle through which much academic writing has viewed the issue of domestic workers.

My interest in looking at the ways in which scholars have portrayed domestic workers is driven by the understanding that research does not only reflect the ways the world is, but also shapes the world in which we live through the act of knowledge production (Graham 2000); hence, research is a performative practice, defined by Butler as "the reiterative and citational practice through which discourse produces the effects that it names" (1993:2). As de Regt (2010) notes, many of the studies that deal with domestic workers in the Middle East focus on the abuse and exploitation, making a plea for the regulation of women's legal status and pointing to oppression and inequality. I argue that the discourse on cases of extreme abuse contributes to the development of a hierarchy of violence, whereby some forms of abuse can be tolerated and others not.

Furthermore, some prominent academic work on migrant domestic workers has framed domestic work in Lebanon and in the Gulf in terms of slavery-like practices (Jureidini and Moukarbel 2004). The modern-day-slavery argument is used to highlight trafficking of the domestic workers, which is linked to the use of force or deception within the migration process and to describe the effects of the *kafala*. The discourse on trafficking constructs the domestic workers as victims and gives legitimacy to states' anti-trafficking measures that encompass draconian anti-migration laws and stringent policing of migrants, which ironically increase trafficking and labor exploitation of undocumented migrants (Andrijasevic 2007). Scholars have highlighted the ways in which anti-trafficking policies and discourses tend to eclipse other forms of abuse within migration and dismiss the rights of the workers to labor entitlements and rights, including the right to organize (Mahdavi 2011). However, one needs to ask which categories of labor are discursively produced as 'slaves' and which are not. Why are some categories made visible under this category and not others? And why are migrant domestic workers produced as the emblematic example of neo-slavery while the Syrian construction workers in Beirut are not? There are few comparative studies that discern the commonalities among domestic workers and other subordinated groups, both urban and rural, under neoliberalism. Some scholars have criticized the slavery discourse, underlining the fact that under neoliberalism the boundary is blurred between 'free' and 'unfree' wage labor and between forced labor and extremely poor working conditions (Davidson 2006; Millar 2014). Other scholars, such as Pande, have argued that the victim discourse produces a category of labor that disciplines workers:

> *The demand for the extension of human rights to MDWs [migrant domestic workers] on the basis of their overarching vulnerability delimits the political potential of workers to resist exploitation and abuses, form alliances, and fight for their own rights. Such third party demands, made on humanitarian grounds, conceal and diminish powerful struggles organized by the workers themselves.* (Pande 2012:385)

The idea here is that migrant domestic workers are perceived solely as objects of biopower of the state, the neoliberal market, and migratory regimes. This construction neglects the everyday array of mechanisms employed by these workers to cope, to negotiate, and even to resist their precarious condition. In fact, in reaction to the victimhood framework, some scholars have undertaken research inspired by James Scott's *Weapons of the Weak* (1985) to analyze covert forms of subversions on the individual and local levels. Some of this work, for instance, has highlighted the everyday resistance, like foot-dragging and mockery, deployed by women in their negotiations with their employers. Moukarbel (2009) explores the ways in which emotional ties with the family members are used by the servant as means to defy the control exercised by the employers. Pande (2012) highlights the "meso-levels" of resistance undertaken by migrant domestics which cannot be classified as either private and individual or as organized collective action. These acts involve strategic dyads forged across balconies by the most restricted live-in workers and small informal communities formed by migrant domestic workers. The focus of this literature on the individual level of resistance is due to the fact that collective organizing continues to be a difficult task due to the nature of the work, because women working in dispersed workplaces have few avenues for interaction with each other.

By exploring the trade-union situation for female and male domestic workers in Lebanon, I hope to move beyond the "weapons of the weak" and contribute to the literature on the collective organizing of migrant domestic workers. However, I want to make it clear that I do not believe that one form of resistance is more legitimate or more important than another. There is no inherent contradiction between the everyday and the organized forms of resistance that gives the social processes their salience (Gutmann 1993). Instead, one needs to ask what makes actors, under what circumstances, follow one or the other form of resistance, and what the relation between them is. These forms regarding domestic workers, as we will see, occur together and transform themselves into each other. Finally, I argue that the union for domestic workers, which alternatively mobilizes their subjectivities as workers, contributes to the recovering of the salience of class in the new economy and to the recognition of domestic work as work like any other. In this regard, the class analysis disrupts the narrative of victimization and offers support for the constitution of new subject positions for migrant domestic workers outside the static constraints of the victim identity.

Research Questions

My interest in the question of domestic workers grew out of my broader interest in the question of labor and labor organizing in Lebanon and in the region. This interest was that of a socialist and a feminist activist who believes that the working class has a central position in the struggle for justice. The ways in which workers, even the most precarious and marginal, find strength in collective and organized struggles has always seized my attention: the strike of tax collectors for equal pay in Egypt in 2008, the Future Pipe factory workers' plant occupation in North Lebanon in 2010, the union for domestic workers in Beirut in 2015, and the dozens of other workers' actions that I have followed. In all of these events that emanated from the experience of distress and injustice, both male and female workers, through their own action, were creating a world of possibilities, of shared strength, solidarity, and affection. I witnessed the same phenomenon during the launching of the trade union for domestic workers, and later during my interviews with them. Their narratives are full of accounts of daily attacks on their integrity and dignity, but they also bear witness to incredible strength and courage, and to the hope they place in social change.

I was involved in the very first stage of the union in 2013, when I was invited by the ILO, as member of the Anti-Racism Movement, to facilitate a question-and-answer session with Ethiopian workers about their shared experience of domestic work. This session was one of many sessions that were taking place at FENASOL with domestic workers from different nationalities, within the Participatory Action Research (PAR) that the ILO designed in close cooperation with domestic workers. This research was the base of what later became the union. My involvement was interrupted when I went to Cairo to study for a master's degree in gender and women's studies. After a year and a half I returned to Lebanon to find that the women who took part in the research had become unionists and were preparing to launch their trade union. One of the things that caught my attention was the transformation that happened on the level of their discourse, from the very personalized experience of abuse during the PAR to the discourse on their collective experience as domestic workers, which was marked by a more assertive claim of their rights as workers. The engagement of these women in labor-union organizing within a Lebanese federation of trade unions led me to pose a series of questions:

1. On the level of the trade-union movement in Lebanon, I ask: What challenges do the informalization, feminization, and internationalization of labor pose for the trade unions?
2. On the level of the women's-rights organizations, I ask: How does the women's movement in Lebanon engage with the question of domestic work?
3. On the level of the militant domestic workers, I ask: What motivates them to organize and to break through the fear and danger surrounding their 'illegal' action? What does the union mean to them? And how they are forging their collective workers' identity?

Theoretical Framework

This research examines how domestic workers in Lebanon are collectively struggling to transform the economic and social conditions of paid domestic work through labor-union organizing. It looks at the ways in which they strive to assert their right to a dignifying existence by redefining their working conditions and the processes that shape their labor and give it meaning. It also studies the effects that their action can have on labor and feminist politics.

In talking about domestic workers we are talking about women, predominantly migrants. Their experience as workers is entangled with other elements that contribute to their subject positioning. In fact, migrant domestic workers experience three-fold exploitation: as migrants, as women, and as workers. The lack of social recognition for domestic workers is due to the fact that it is considered an extension of women's natural role. This lack of recognition is coupled with an intensified degradation of the occupation through its association with race and nationality (Jureidini 2009). Gutierrez-Rodríguez argues that "while this labor is constitutive for the production of value, this value is largely not recognized in society because the cultural predication of this labor connotes it as 'non-productive' and its labor force is devalued through its prescription as feminized and racialized labor" (Gutierrez-Rodríguez 2010:8). Indeed, the relative positioning of migrant domestic workers is shaped by their relations to capital, gender, and race. I employ class as an analytical tool to analyze the labor union for domestic workers in relation to the labor-union movement and the women's rights movement in Lebanon. Class, however, is understood as a process rather than a fixed structure to which one belongs (Graham 2000). It is understood as a relation that is open to constant transformations. This understanding of class helps enlightening the ways in which it articulates with other aspects of social existence, as in the case of migrant domestic workers, and allows us to see the constant change in the composition of the working class and labor relations with the development of capitalism. How can we then understand class and labor organizing in the neoliberal age of precarity and informality of labor?

Paid domestic workers attest to the ways in which capital expansion has brought new labor categories under capitalist relations. Broader structural changes in capitalism have weakened the link between capital and labor, thereby displacing the industrial working class of the Fordist model with a more fragmented and segmented multitude whose relationship to work and production is more tenuous. Different terms have arisen in the past two decades in order to give a meaning and a name to the contemporary labor experiences under neoliberalism. 'Informality' is commonly used in labor theories to describe labor trends characterized, as Arnold and Bongiovi put it, by a growing "decline in attachment to employers, an increase in long-term unemployment, growth in perceived and real job insecurity, increasing nonstandard and contingent work, risk shifting from employers to employees, a lack of workplace safety, and an increase in work-based stress and harassment" (Arnold and Bongiovi 2013:290). Other authors define informality in different ways; however, it is generally understood as remunerative work that is not recognized, regulated, or protected by existing legal or regulatory frameworks, as well as non-remunerative work undertaken in an income-generating enterprise (Arnold and Bongiovi 2013).

In fact, these labor trends, which are in no way new but follow previous patterns, have created new barriers to labor organizing. The post-Fordist transformations under the neoliberal shift—that is, the flexibilization of production systems and its implications for labor informalization—have led to the weakening of workers' collective bargaining power. The membership losses of trade unions could also be attributed to their reluctance to reach out beyond the formal, workplace-based, male-dominated workers (Kabeer, Milward, and Sudarshan 2013). Although many trade unions have incorporated 'renewal projects' to respond to these recent challenges and increasingly address the issues of the 'unorganized,' these projects tend to "defend, rather than rethink, the traditional labor movement" (Chang 2012:45). In other words, these projects are still considered as "additional work for the labor movement" rather than deep "reorientation" (Chang 2009:177). New centers of labor struggles have, paradoxically, erupted with the expanding circuits of capitalist production and its modalities of accumulation. In this sense, the processes of fragmentation and segmentation of the working class, which were partially intended to dilute contradictions and weaken the bargaining power of labor, have shaped the recent mobilizations of the working class. Hence, the migrant domestic workers, who constitute one discrete category of labor, started to organize. Their organizing can be understood as a struggle to transform the class processes that shape their labor as domestic workers and to challenge racial and gender associations with such work. In other words, they are struggling to break free from what some scholars have termed slavery-like conditions. Their union aims to transform paid domestic labor, to displace negative stereotypes, and to confront the dominant ideologies of race, class, and gender. With their assertiveness, a new subjectivity associated with the model of the militant unionist is being forged.

This understanding of the complex construction of subjectivities of domestic workers is not always recognized by labor unions, who have historically mobilized over the formal class model (the industrial/formal male worker), and which are known for their nationalist and exclusionary practices toward migrants. Hence, the domestic workers were not perceived by the unions historically as workers worth organizing. On the contrary, they were invisible, or, at best, considered marginal temporary workers in a devalued labor process; hence their labor dimension was disregarded. It is rather ironic that this category of labor, among other informal workers, that was historically shunned by the trade unions is today seen as the one on which the future (and present) survival of the trade-union movement is based. At this level, there is a need for the trade unions to adopt alternative discourse and strategies to deal with a growing feminized, internationalized, and informalized labor force. In this regard, I embrace Papadopoulos and Stephenson's (2008) call for a new form of unionism that operates on transnational and trans-sectorial levels, and which questions the predominant work-force identity as male and native.

Women's-rights organization, on their part, which have also historically prioritized the 'Lebanese woman' in their agenda, started a decade ago to develop programs for domestic workers. However, these organizations dealt with only one aspect of the experience of domestic workers: as female victims of violence. In this framework, not only is the labor dimension of domestic workers ignored, but the deployed violence framework was not questioned. Do all women suffer from the same kind of violence? What about the violence that is exercised by women employers against the women domestic workers? What about the social hierarchies that structure the encounter between these two categories of women? As Gibson-Graham argues, the household represents a "social site in which a wide variety of class, gender, racial, sexual and other practices intersect" (Gutierrez-Rodríguez 2010:10). However, in the framework of the women's-rights organizations, only the gender aspect is stressed. This gender identification works to subsume and conceal differences of race and class.

Fieldwork and Methodology

My fieldwork was conducted between December 2014 and February 2015. It consisted of 15 one-on-one interviews, informal meetings, small group discussions with members and non-members of the migrant domestic workers' union, and participatory observations, which took place at FENASOL's headquarters and other workers' gatherings, such as the union congress. I conducted seven in-depth interviews with the members of the executive board of the union for domestic workers including workers from Lebanon, the Philippines, Sri Lanka, Cameroon, and Madagascar; economists; Lebanese trade unionists from FENASOL and the CGTL; women's-rights activists from Kafa; and ILO officials.

Although I had previously been involved in the preliminary stages of the union for domestic workers, my positioning vis-à-vis those with whom I interacted in the course of this research was not always defined strictly by this relationship. My interactions with various Lebanese union activists, in particular, were all closely tied to my previous work with the Lebanese Labor Watch (a center for the defense of workers' rights). When meeting with them, I always made a point of explaining the academic objective of my work and that it was not linked to any NGO work. This careful reminder of my academic objective proved to be important as a strategy to obtain access to FENASOL's headquarters, but not to the extent of allowing me to attend the board meetings of the union for domestic workers. The objections to my frequent requests to attend these meetings were mediated by the unspoken sensitivities of the NGOs and FENASOL over migrant domestic workers' organizing and representation. Despite the fact that the union was born out of the cooperation between some NGOs, FENASOL, and the ILO, the relations among these groups were nonetheless characterized by tension. I was told by some of my interlocutors that some NGOs consider themselves to be the 'godfathers' of migrant domestic workers, since their long years of engagement with them had given them more expertise in dealing with them, while the labor unions were newcomers to this field and lacked expertise in dealing with migrant women. FENASOL's leadership, for its part, considers that the 'natural' place of the domestic workers, as workers, is in the labor unions. Its leadership agrees that the NGOs' involvement was very fruitful in advancing the cause of domestic workers; however, they lack the expertise, the ability, and the desire to collectively organize the workers. Hence the tension is the result of competition over representation of domestic workers, driven by donor funding, that rendered the migrant domestic workers a valuable asset to be fought over among groups such as NGOs and unions. It also highlights the ways in which the different actors position them as workers, as women, and as migrants. For instance, in the union context they are mainly considered workers; for Kafa they are migrant women. Thus my previous work with some NGOs was to a certain extent conflated with my new 'hat' as researcher in the eyes of FENASOL's leadership, and it influenced the ways they perceived me.

My interactions with members of the migrant domestic workers' union mostly took place outside FENASOL's headquarters. We met in various cafés and restaurants in Beirut. The workers were aware of my work on workers' rights, or at the very least my relations and previous engagement with the Anti-Racism Movement and the feminist organization Nasawiya, which were involved in migrant workers' community organizing. This element, contrary to my experience with FENASOL's leadership, facilitated my interactions with the migrant domestic workers, who identified me as a Lebanese ally. As Sangster (1994) suggests, one's past and current political ideologies shape the construction of the interviews and the narrative form. For example, the shared political and ethical commitments represented an affinity through which the workers felt comfortable sharing with me their opinions and feelings, and sometimes soliciting my personal opinion regarding issues related to their union. I was aware of the working of my privilege throughout my fieldwork as a researcher vis-à-vis my interlocutors. In fact, I was struggling with an ethical dilemma related to the researcher's authority and ability to easily access the most intimate aspects of the lives of less privileged people. As Stacey notes: "Fieldwork represents an intrusion and intervention into a system of relationships that the researcher is far freer than the researched to leave" (1988:23). In fact, simply by virtue of being

researchers we occupy a position of authority that allows us to inter-
pret and control the outcomes. While I share Sangster's view that it is
impossible to create "an ideal feminist methodology that negates power
differences" (1994:12), I still believe that there is a way to reduce the
power gap between researcher and interviewees and render research a
more democratic endeavor. This remedy is influenced by Enslin (1994),
who lays the groundwork for an alternative praxis of ethnography (feminist ethnography in particular), whereby practice and theory are put
under constant critical assessment through direct involvement of the
researcher in his/her community under study. This engagement has the
potential of transforming research and rendering the researcher politically accountable before his/her interlocutors.

    In my interviews with domestic workers I was particularly inter-
ested in gathering their personal narratives, their history of organizing,
their motivations to join the union, their relation to the NGOs, and
their perception of labor-union activism. The majority of the women
interviewed constitute the most active militants in the newly formed
union. They have been in Lebanon between seven and 30 years. They are
freelancers, which means that they live on their own and they can chose
the employer they wish to work for. In other words, while they are still
governed by the *kafala*, they have established relations of trust with their
kafeel which allowed them to have greater mobility. Most of them have
a history in community organizing before the union and some of them
have university degrees; at least one of them was a schoolteacher before
migrating to Lebanon. The women spoke either French or English, and
in both cases we were able to communicate without a translator. Their
narratives made me realize that there is no one category of domestic
workers, and that domestic work is differently lived and experienced
based on employment conditions (freelance, live-in), nationality, age,
education, and language proficiency. These different experiences also
shaped the women workers' activism and trade-union militancy.

CHAPTER 2

Workers without Trade Unions, Trade Unions without Workers

The Working Class Is Dead, Long Live the Working Class

"There is no working class any more in Lebanon," says Ahmad, a 63-year-old university professor who was a labor agitator in the Ghandour Candy Company in the early 1970s and who was affiliated with the Communist Action Organization. The Ghandour factory once employed over 1,300 workers and is still entrenched in the collective memory of the Left as a leading site for labor activism prior to the civil war, following the major 1972 strike that ended with the police killing two workers, Fatma Khawaja and Yusuf Attar. In the post–civil war era, the factory was split into two smaller factories, following a dispute among the heirs. Today, one of the two factories employs 80 Lebanese and migrant workers on a contract basis, and the other, which was relocated to Saudi Arabia, employs around 200 workers. What has happened with the Ghandour factory workers is somehow representative of the transformations that occurred at the level of the labor force in Lebanon, which pushed some observers to lament the 'death' of the working class.

The myth of the demise of the working class is widely accepted in Lebanese society and propagated equally by its secular and sectarian elite on all points of the political spectrum, on the left and on the right. The myth holds that people living within this geographical space of 10,452 square kilometers are made up exclusively of sectarian communities, not social classes. I agree with Traboulsi that this is in fact a myth, one that acts to conceal social disparities within the society: "The denial of the existence of class comes as no surprise. Every social system exercises its own special logic when it comes to concealing manifestations of privilege, inequality and exploitation between its members" (Traboulsi 2014:6). Against the idea that 'class is dead,' I would argue that there is a need for a theory and praxis of class politics that do not see only formal factory workers as representatives of the working class, who remain until today the object of leftist nostalgia. In this sense, I treat class as dynamic social relations that are not fixed, nor always easy to identify. Rather, I perceive class relations as shaped largely by the changes in relations of production under neoliberalism.

In fact, the neoliberal turn since the 1970s has dramatically reconfigured the working class. With it, profound changes have occurred on the level of relations of productions, labor practices, and organization. The working class has come under considerable economic pressure, which has limited its political power (Hardt 1996). The fragmentation of production processes and the pursuit of flexible labor market strategies have replaced the concentrated and stable labor force with a "disaggregated, dispersed, largely informal and increasingly female labor force" (Kabeer, Milward, and Sudarshan 2013:4). Thus, entire labor categories that once enjoyed certain stability have found themselves in precarious employment conditions. Moreover, the flexible and diffuse flow of capital corresponded with a constant deterritorialization and reterritorialization of labor. Structural adjustments programs, economic and political crises, and international trade agreements have had devastating consequences on the global south, driving labor to migrate, sometimes legally but often illegally, in search of better life opportunities, not just in the North but also to sites of capital investment such as Singapore, Beijing, and Rio, and to resource extraction industries in Africa. However, while the South–North labor migration has occupied a central place in the scholarship, South–South migration is understudied, even though it is equally significant (de Regt 2010; Ong 2006). Gutierrez-Rodríguez (2007) argues that, even today, coloniality of power continues to mark the patterns of contemporary transnational migration. This entails the hierarchal classification, and the gendered and racial differentiation, of populations from the South in the labor market who occupy the most 'undesirable' jobs. Driven by the logic of capital accumulation, a process of devaluation of labor takes place, which is reflected in their exploitation as racialized and feminized labor.

Under these circumstances, traditional trade unions that are based on the Fordist model of organizing are facing serious challenges. The contemporary conditions of the working class require new means of organizing, new ways of forging alliances to advance workers' political power, and creative strategies of resistance, or what Foucault calls "counter-conducts" (cited in Lazzarato 2009:114). This alliance must transcend the segmentation of professions, qualifications, nationality, race, ethnicity, and gender that are exacerbated and promoted by the dominant classes. However, the fact remains that trade unions in Lebanon, and globally, perpetuate the national ethnocentric analysis of labor and continue to organize following the Fordist model of the formal, male-breadwinner worker. Vast categories of labor, such as informal migrant women, are overlooked by trade-union movements. In many instances they are scapegoated for economic crises, job scarcity, and unemployment. In Lebanon and elsewhere, under neoliberalism, the situation can be summarized in one sentence: there are workers without trade unions, and trade unions without workers.

This chapter aims to situate the union for domestic workers within the context of the labor-union 'movement' in Lebanon. Working within private spaces, domestic workers may be relatively invisible. But numbering nearly 200,000, they constitute one of the largest sectors of Lebanon's working class, and represent one of the changing faces of labor relations under neoliberalism. Unionizing domestic workers opens up the discussion on the possibility of organizing those who are perceived as unorganizable. But it also suggests that, under the current neoliberal order, labor unions cannot continue to ignore these 'excessive' laboring bodies who are increasingly informal, migrants, and women.

Neoliberalism and Precarious Labor

The founding ideology of the Lebanese state, still in place today, is that for the country to function, it needs a certain amount of state power to guarantee the status of the sectarian communities as mediators with the individual citizens, and a great deal of 'laissez-faire' economy. The Lebanese constitution, adopted in 1926, is one of the rare constitutions that specify the economic system of the country. It states: "The economic system is free and ensures private initiative and the right of private property" (article 6). This does not mean that the state does not intervene in the economy. On the contrary, "this intervention for social redistribution of the wealth comes not from the upper social classes in favor of the ones down, but from down in favor of the upper social classes," according to Fawwaz Traboulsi in a lecture. He adds:

Examples are numerous: the tax system that favors the rich, the subsidies that the Lebanese government provides for the private sector including private schools and hospitals—not to speak of the fact that the structure of the Lebanese economy favors, first, the banking sector; second, the real-estate sector, and third, the import trade. What I mean is that in Lebanon and elsewhere under neoliberalism, and against the common belief, the state does intervene a lot in the economy, but in the interest of the wealthy. The peculiarity, however, is that the Lebanese state was initially a liberal economic state since independence. What happened is that we moved from the liberalism of the prewar period to the neoliberalism of the postwar period. (Traboulsi 2015)

The post–civil war Lebanese economy of the 1990s experienced a pronounced free-market neoliberalization coupled with labor deregulation (Picard 2013). The rent economic model that was enforced demanded a low-paid foreign working force that would not constitute a burden on capital. At the same time, beginning even before the civil war, it encouraged the Lebanese labor force to migrate to the neighboring Gulf countries that were witnessing a boom in oil prices, guaranteeing a continuous flow of financial remittances (personal interview, M. Zbeeb, January 2015). Tabar (2010) highlights the ways in which families in Lebanon became largely dependent on remittances, which constituted 88 percent of household savings and 22 percent of household income. He argues that this money is what allows the society to cope with the lack of proper social and welfare services (Tabar 2010:17). The rent economy has been put in place to serve a surrounding economy floating in oil money. While the service, financial, and banking sectors were growing, the shares of agriculture and industry in the economy were shrinking. Tabar argues that the economically hegemonic class in Lebanon, "which is communally and traditionally fragmented, has refused to develop its agrarian and industrial sectors. Instead, it concentrated on the tertiary sector, placing emphasis on trading, tourism, banking and finance. This trend has been reinforced since 1990 as a result of the commitment of successive governments to neo-liberal economic policies, leading to a limited labor market characterized by low pay" (2010:6). Parallel to that, an informal economy has been growing consistently, which the International Monetary Fund (IMF) has estimated at 30 percent of GDP.[1] A structural deformation in the economy took place following the civil war, as medium and small enterprises came to dominate. A survey conducted in 2003 found that 97 percent of these enterprises employ fewer than ten workers, and 46.8 percent employ between two and four workers, while businesses with only one employee account for almost 45 percent (Hamdan 2003).

The situation has been no better for the workers. Millar (2014) underlines the shared experience of precarity common to labor under neoliberalism, in which the availability and conditions of work are unstable and under which temporary and irregular labor exist in a constant state of anxiety, desperation, and risk. Indeed, in Lebanon a broad segment of the workers have been turned into precarious contract workers who live day by day, without even minimal security. Half of the workers residing in Lebanon are not covered by any healthcare provisions, and despite popular demands, the government still refuses to discuss a project for universal health care. In addition, three-quarters of the labor force is not covered by a pension plan, nor do they have any form of unemployment benefits. The rate of salaried work in formal sectors has declined considerably, to 29 percent of the labor force.[2] The public sector and state administrations are filled with thousands of day and contract workers (Lebanese Labor Watch 2013). It is clear that neoliberal economic policies have conscripted the majority of the workers residing in Lebanon into precarious living conditions, in the service of the minority that benefit from it.

In fact, the post–civil war environment in Lebanon has constituted a major challenge for trade unions. The latter have been unable to constitute a force that could produce effective change in the economy, or at

---

1 "IMF: Lebanon's Informal Economy 30 Percent of GDP," *The Daily Star*, November 2, 2011. http://www.dailystar.com.lb/Business/Lebanon/2011/Nov-02/152829-imf-lebanons-informal-economy-30-percent-of-gdp.ashx.

2 M. Zbeeb, "A Nation Living Day to Day," *al-Akhbar English*, May 31, 2012, http://english.al-akhbar.com/node/7917.

least to restore balance to the unequal power relations between increasingly impoverished segments of the population and the governing
coalition (business elite, traditional elite, and warlords who ascended
to power following the Ta'if agreement that put an end to the civil war
[1975–1990]). To the contrary, the trade unions, and at their center
the General Confederation of Lebanese Workers (CGTL)—the sole
officially recognized representative of workers in Lebanon—came out
of the war weak, less militant, more porous to sectarian divisions and
political parties' control, more conservative, less democratic, and less
radical than ever, as Zbeeb puts it: "The current leadership (of the
CGTL) has played a deliberate role in thwarting any serious challenge to the imbalance of power between workers and employers in
Lebanon. Ever since an alliance of warlords and big money assumed
control of the Lebanese state under Syrian tutelage, the CGTL has
become a key tool for taming society."[3]

Trade Unions without Workers

In the postwar years, the government needed to silence the trade-
union movement in order to implement its neoliberal policies with the
least opposition possible. At that time, in the mid 1990s, the CGTL
was led by a militant left-leaning leadership that opposed government policies creating a high public debt, large trade and budgetary
deficits, and growing impoverishment of workers and wage earners
(Baroudi 1998). One of the trade unions' main demands was wage
increases for public and private sectors to compensate workers for the
loss in purchasing power resulting from inflation in 1992. One of the
main strategies used by the Ministry of Labor to curb the militancy of
the movement was the granting of permissions (licenses) for 'yellow'
trade-union federations—that is, federations set up and controlled by
political parties and state officials—and to push for their inclusion
in the CGTL executive council in order to prevent the election of
anti-government candidates to the leadership of the confederation
and to control its decision-making process and strategies. In fact, the
Labor Code allows for a group of three or more trade unions to form
a federation. The latter can have two representatives on the executive
council of the CGTL, regardless of its membership size. Thus, the

---

3 Zbeeb, "A Nation Living Day to Day."

Trade Union for Workers in the Paper Products Factories, which has 142 members, has two representatives, the same as the Trade Union of Banks' Employees, which has 10,000 members.

By 'spawning' yellow trade unions, the government succeeded in hijacking the CGTL. Although this policy dates from before the war it became more pronounced in the 1990s as the government grew stronger and more determined to implement its neoliberal project. Baroudi writes: "Upon coming to power, Hariri[4] adopted a tougher stance towards unions because he objected to their tactics and feared that their 'exaggerated demands' for higher wages and more fringe benefits would jeopardize his economic reform program" (Baroudi 1998:544). For example, in 1997, in order to oust the militant leadership of the CGTL, the Ministry of Labor licensed the creation of seven new federations loyal to the Speaker of the House and the leader of the Amal Movement, admitting them to the CGTL despite being rejected by its leadership. Consequently, the CGTL grew from nine federations of trade unions in 1970, to 21 in 1993, to 28 in 1997, to 37 in 2000, to 50 federations of trade unions today, comprising 600 affiliated trade unions (Badran and Zbeeb 2011). This inflation in the number of trade unions did not correspond to growth in their membership. On the contrary, a study that was done in 2000, based on the official elections lists presented to the Ministry of Labor, estimated the total membership of all federations of trade unions around 58,000. This means that the actual representation of the CGTL does not exceed, at best, 7 percent of the total Lebanese labor force (Badran and Zbeeb 2011). In the absence of more recent statistics, many trade unionists and labor activists argue that, most likely, in the last ten years there has been a decline in trade-union membership, especially with the weakening of the CGTL's position, its lack of actions, and its inability to achieve any of the demands raised by its member unions for over a decade. Since the state succeeded in defeating the militant leadership of the CGTL in 1997, the CGTL has become an organization that maintains the status quo rather than

---

4 Rafik Hariri was a businessman of great influence. He headed five cabinets as prime minister of Lebanon from 1992 until his assassination in 2005. He came to power with an economic program that had a definite order of priorities: reversing the deterioration of the foreign exchange rate for the Lebanese lira, curbing inflation, and launching a massive reconstruction program.

challenging it. The many instances in which the CGTL betrayed workers' interests, as well as its open alliance with political parties in power, distanced workers from union politics. The reduced influence of workers is also related to the fact that the CGTL has become a proactive player in the political/sectarian division in the society. Apart from its usual recourse to union leaders in order to settle disputes between a worker and the management, the CGTL and its affiliated unions contributed very little to collective negotiations and workplace agitations. Union elections at CGTL were thus largely based on the politics of personal allegiances, in which the workers elected their representatives in order to provide a direct connection to union leaders that they could make use of when necessary. The CGTL became a corporatist body which is organized hierarchically, with power concentrated at the top of the hierarchy. Rather than an institution representing workers, it has become an instrument fostering the interests of the state. While the CGTL had previously built its membership base among workers in the formal sector, today, more than ever, the workers in the informal economy constitute the next challenge for the trade-union movement.

Workers without Trade Unions

The informal sector accounts for half of the labor force in Lebanon. The common feature of informal employment is the level of precarity for the workers involved. Precarity is an important framework for mobilizing people who have traditionally been located outside of the margins of trade-union organizing, such as women and migrants (Arnold and Bongiovi 2013). The concept of precarity has been used in the literature on labor "both as an analytical tool and as a strategic point of departure to produce political subjectivities and re-invent different alliances and ways of struggle" (Casas-Cortés, in Arnold and Bongiovi 2013:299). Kabeer argues: "Workers' organizations tend to articulate their strategies, forms and modes of organizing around well-defined work places, tasks and employers, and around a model of the worker as breadwinner man. Informal sector workers, on the other hand, may have physically dispersed workplaces, a wide range of tasks, no identifiable employer, and, increasingly women" (Kabeer, Milward, and Sudarshan 2013:4). Some of the characteristics of informality are lack of protection in the event of non-payment of wages, compulsory overtime, layoffs without notice or compensation, unsafe working conditions, and the absence of social benefits and social security. At the same time, informal-sector workers pose serious challenges to trade unions. Despite the growing number of informal-sector workers, the attitude of the trade unions toward them has been, and still is, often characterized by fear and hostility, since they are perceived as a threat to the privileges they have won through their organized action. In the next section I cite one example of this 'hostility' against informal workers that I was following as a labor activist and journalist in 2012.

At the beginning of May 2012 the contract workers of EDL (Électricité du Liban), Lebanon's public electric company, declared a strike, demanding permanent employment, fairer wages, and social and health security. They held their protest inside the EDL building and its courtyard, halting all work inside the company. The workers wanted the state to recognize that they had been working informally and in the shadow of the company for many years, and that the injuries some workers suffered in the course of their highly risky jobs (especially for repair workers) had not been compensated. The strikers were also making a statement against the privatization of the company, arguing that it would take away their rights, their social security, and other benefits. The strike continued for 94 days, one of the longest strikes in the modern history of Lebanon. During this entire time, the workers were able to maintain their unity despite state repression and harassment. The workers were pressured to end their strike following the so-called 'political agreement' sponsored by the Hezbollah party, the Amal movement (two Shia parties to which many of the workers belong), the Free Patriotic Movement (a Christian party established by Michel Aoun, an army general, to which the minister of energy and water belongs), and the umbrella of the CGTL (to which no one belongs). The agreement was based on an immediate cessation of the strike in return for a 'promise' that the workers would obtain the status of full-time employees. The result was that the workers ended their strike. The promise of full employment evaporated. Three private companies (service providers) started operating in the EDL over which the workers were distributed on a contract basis, resulting in the loss of their bargaining power.

On one level, the CGTL's betrayal of the workers and the lack of union representation made the negotiations between the management and the workers mediated and dependent on workers' relations within their political parties. "We were left to face the Minister of Energy and Water alone, without any support of the CGTL; we felt that we were orphaned throughout the 94 days," a leader of the strike told me. Indeed, the EDL contract workers did not get any kind of support from the CGTL throughout the strike. The latter intervened on the last day to put an end to the strike in close coordination with the sectarian political parties in power, which were more interested in having a share in the partial privatization deal that resulted than in advancing the workers' interests.

On another level, the trade union of the EDL employees held an aggressive position toward the contract workers and sided with the minister and the EDL management. During the strike, the trade union hung leaflets on the walls and doors of the company stating that the strike was "inhibiting the flow of work in the company and obstructing the interests of the citizens." At the time, one of the strikers told me: "If the union had taken a stand in support of our strike, we would have won, and we would have guaranteed our rights and the rights of the full-time employees in light of the growing threat of gradual privatization of the company and the gradual attack on the rights of the workers." The EDL contract workers' case is only one example of the ways in which formal trade unions and the CGTL deal with informal workers. The latter are not only distant from their agenda and outreach, but are also ignored and treated with hostility.

Women and Trade Unions: A Conflicted Relationship

Women and trade unions have often had a conflicted history. In fact, the early history of trade unions was marked by the exclusion of women workers. Societal representations of women and of their roles hindered their organization into a coherent force for change. For instance, Malek Abisaab argues that in the 1920s the trade-union leaders' outlook and organizational strategies undermined gender differences in the labor force (2010:17). Further, he argues that

> *The lack of emphasis on demands particular to women forced the latter at times to take an independent course of action and march out against the government without the help of union leaders or working-men. The unionists and communists, on their part, did not seriously*

investigate the strong female-based agendas, one of which addressed domestic work and child care as a critical dimension of what women's labor entailed. They did not attempt to seek women-friendly strategies for recruitment or women-friendly schedules for labor organization meetings. Instead, male-tailored language, planning practices, and mobilization of initiatives prevailed. (Abisaab 2010:18)

For these reasons, women's early expressions of labor activism were not born out of unionism, but emanated from their own experiences of exploitation at work. They managed to create a significant labor militancy history of their own, beginning with the early silk factories in the nineteenth century in Mount Lebanon, which were based largely on women's labor (Khater 1996). Upon the decline of the previously highly lucrative silk industry, the tobacco industry expanded considerably with the establishment in 1935 of the French tobacco monopoly, the Régie Co-Intéressée Libanaise des Tabacs et Tombacs, with a female work force amounting to 40 percent. Abissaab shows the ways in which women were the most proactively radical, specifically during the 1946 labor strike in which they protested the Régie's discriminatory labor practices. Their activism, the author argues, resulted in the passage of the Labor Law for all workers that, while imperfect, was nevertheless a historic step in their struggle. However, women's contribution to the Lebanese labor movement was only faintly acknowledged by labor historians as well as unionists and communists. The scarce historical records—such as in al-'Aris (1982) and al-Buwari (1986), two prominent pioneering historians of the Lebanese trade-union movement—left out most of the labor struggles of working women, mainly because many of these struggles fell outside the realm of 'organized labor.'

Today, despite the fact that the number of women in formal and informal work forces has increased significantly, the unions remain unwilling to rework their structures and strategies to accommodate the new labor force. The growing numbers of women in paid work has not led to their unionization. Thus, women continue to remain underrepresented in the activities and leadership of all labor unions in Lebanon. Among the 100 representatives of the 50 federations of trade unions in the executive council of the CGTL, there is not one single woman representative.

A series of internal challenges associated with unions themselves have hindered the participation, organization, and representation of women workers. A male-dominated culture within mainstream unions makes it easy to overlook woman-specific issues. This culture also tends to blame the woman for her underrepresentation in the unions. Reflecting on this issue, Castro Abdallah, the president of FENASOL, says:

As FENASOL we are better than the other labor federations because at least we pay a little attention to women. Historically, we had female membership in the sewing sector, the printing sector, and the tobacco cultivation sector. But there's still a problem in women's membership, and women are the ones who bear the responsibility because they lock themselves in at work. They don't interact with other coworkers. We tried to impose a law in 1982 that stipulates that at least one woman should sit on the executive board of the Federation and each union's branch, and the law established a women's committee. However, once we couldn't find a woman to run for the women's committee representative seat, so a man took it. There's another problem related to the fact that old men in the Federation wouldn't give up their seats for women working in their sectors. The mentality of the male unionists is that if women don't want to join the unions, why should we address them or encourage them to do so? After all, that will ease our burden as unionists. Others ask: why should we call on women to join when they will ultimately compete for our seats? Also, women have not imposed themselves on the unions. On the one hand, women are forgotten by the unions; on the other hand, even when the unions paved the way for them to enter, the women didn't take the initiative to push the door and open it. (Personal interview with Castro Abdallah, president of FENASOL, February 2015)

FENASOL is the oldest communist federation of labor unions that grew historically out of working-class struggles against capitalism and colonialism in the 1930s. Following years of repression, persecution, and incarceration of its leaders because of their "communist activities" (Bou Habib 2011), the Federation was finally granted a government license in 1966. It became a member of the CGTL in 1970 and withdrew its membership in 2012. Following the civil-war era, however, FENASOL did not escape the fate of the overall labor movement in the country. In fact, the war, coupled with a growing trade-union bureaucracy, undermined the basis of the work of the trade unions.

The distance between the working class and their unions has grown consistently over the past few decades. The goal of the Federation's bureaucrats became the preservation of their 'seats,' even when there were no more members to preside over. The union leadership has become a class of old Lebanese bureaucratic middle-class men who prefer the certainties of established routines to the risks of struggle and recruitment of new union members. Keeping women out of the unions despite the fact that it weakens all workers (including male workers) reflects the norms of the male-centered union bureaucracy. Indeed, the labor unions have suffered, and continue to suffer, from structural problems related to their lack of labor membership, from inadequate internal democratic decision-making mechanisms, and finally from their lack of independence from sectarian political interventions. These structural problems turned the labor unions into calcified bureaucratic bodies that act as a major obstacle to women's membership specifically, but also to migrant workers.

The Migrant as the 'Other'

Since 1990, Lebanon has increasingly become a 'receiving' country of both Arab and non-Arab migration. Palestinian refugees and migrants from different ethnic groups from Syria and Iraq came to Lebanon long before 1990 and have settled in the country (Tabar 2010). Syrian migrant workers have historically presented a long pattern of inflow migration, ever since Lebanon and Syria emerged as separate nation-states. Tabar argues that the pattern of Syrian inflow migration was facilitated by the ease in transport, short geographic distance, social networking, and the relatively open border between the two countries. Since the end of the war in the 1990s, and the signing of the Ta'if Agreement, Syrians have come to form a large part of the menial labor force in the country. There are also large numbers of migrants from Asia and Africa employed as domestic workers. A 2011 World Bank report states that migrant workers account for 760,000 of a total work force in Lebanon of 1.2 million (in a population of around 4.2 million), predominantly concentrated in the informal sector. This means that migrants constitute more than half of the work force and 17.8 percent of the population. These figures pre-date the large wave of Syrian refugees into Lebanon who fled the Syrian regime's war against the popular uprisings in 2011.

Tabar's article shows the ways in which Lebanon, since its inception, has been a 'sending' country that encourages the outflow migration of its citizens to benefit from their remittances and counts on migration inflow to do the menial labor the Lebanese will no longer do. "The types of jobs that these migrants usually undertake are those jobs that tend to be tough, that retain a certain amount of hazard, and that can be con-sidered dirty" (Shahnawaz 2002). Lebanese nationals are less likely to be hired in these positions, as they are less willing to suffer the indigni-ties of a socially stigmatized, underpaid, and degrading job (Shahnawaz 2002). In fact, migrants are usually hired in "specific economic niches (such as construction and sanitation), in which most Lebanese do not tend to seek employment . . . and therefore do not pose a direct threat to the Lebanese economy or the Lebanese workforce" (Tabar 2010:15).

Despite what Tabar calls the "replacement migration paradigm" (2010:10), trade unions in Lebanon continue to organize along national lines. This phenomenon is not unique to the Lebanese labor unions. Its roots go back to the dominant ideology held by postcolonial coun-tries that privileged a national market that guarantees self-fulfillment, a strong national industry, and a national labor force. This is why even the trade-union bylaws continue to operate along the same lines, linking membership rights to nationality. The migrant workers were given the right to become simple members of the trade unions without having the right to run for elections or vote. To date, the trade unions' discourse, as well as their internal bylaws, do not engage the development of transna-tional workers' mobility and the open-market policies that have brought a large number of foreign workers to the country.

With the growing number of Syrian refugees and workers, both right- and left-wing trade unions called on the Lebanese government and the Ministry of Labor to intervene in order to put an end to the 'competition' between Lebanese and foreign workers and to protect the Lebanese workers. This anti-migration discourse represents a strategy for governing labor and also shapes the nationalist premise of the labor unions. In 2015, the government imposed visa requirements on Syrian nationals for the first time in Lebanon–Syria history, which drastically limited the Syrian inflow migration. This policy was preceded by a Ministry of Labor decree that limited the work that can be done by Syrians to three sectors: agriculture, cleaning, and construction.

The discourse propagated by the trade unions consistently divides the working class into two hostile camps: the national working class and the migrant working class that is accused of lowering the citizens' living standards. This antagonism is intensified by the dominant discourse of the right-wing political parties along with their affiliated media stations regarding Syrian refugees, blaming them for economic, social, and security failures. By the same means, they forge a xenophobic and racist popular opinion against the migrant workers. The *gharib* or the alien (Syrian or Palestinian) is always mobilized in the political discourse in order to bring cohesion to the Lebanese national identity. I agree with Peteet when she notes that the "the Palestinian presence, perceived as a problem, can and does serve as a common denominator in unifying often disparate elements of the Lebanese polity" (Peteet 1996:27). What Peteet describes in relation to the Palestinians is also true for other *ghoraba'a* (plural of *gharib*) in Lebanon. Adding to this xenophobic discourse is a lack of legal protection for migrant workers. "The legal framework excludes the migrant groups from all domains of life —most importantly the labor force" (Tabar 2010:10).

These factors leave the migrant workers open to all sorts of capital exploitation. A precarious residency status coupled with precarious working conditions characterize in particular the low-paid, feminized, and racialized labor sectors. The lack of regulation of employment conditions, in particular in the construction, agriculture, cleaning, and service sectors, means that migrant workers are constantly vulnerable to exploitation. Institutional racism and racist discourse, which go hand in hand with the inflow of migrant workers, act to preserve the operating of a cheap labor market and exploitation. The institutional racism upheld by laws and procedures such as the *kafala* governing migrant workers, and mechanisms of incarceration and deportation, constitute the Schmittian notion reformulated by Agamben on the state of exception that implies a decision by the sovereign to place certain subjects outside the boundaries of the polis. Meanwhile, the trade unions are not interested in defending migrant workers against their fragile working conditions or their exploitability. The unions mention them only as a source of competition with the 'natives.' The state is continuously solicited to regulate and limit the flow of migrant workers that are presumed to be 'competing' and 'stealing' the jobs of the Lebanese.

Trade unionists are not interested in defending the rights of migrant workers on a common ground with Lebanese workers. They are reluctant to build political alliances across differences in order to challenge both the exploitation of migrant workers in the labor market and the class relations that are constructed within capitalism through the practices and processes of racism, sexism, and even sectarianism.

Conclusion

This chapter has examined the structural problems of the trade-union movement in Lebanon since the end of the civil war in 1990. These problems add to the pressing economic difficulties that were made deeper by the neoliberal policies of the coalition in power. From the 1990s onward, the already weakened trade-union movement had to face many challenges. Government intervention in the labor movement succeeded in subjugating the movement—not just the CGTL at its core, but also other federations that present themselves as alternatives to the CGTL, such as FENASOL. The unions lost their independence and their ability to represent the working class. Hence, a reconfigured and a less conflictual labor movement has been the product of the post–civil war era, and it is within this context that the union for domestic workers has come to light.

CHAPTER 3

The Missing Worker in "Domestic Worker": Class Politics and Women's-Rights Organizations

We may unite with Lebanese women who have the same problems as us; for example, the Lebanese women working in the same sector as us. I am speaking about working-class women, but women in the city, I do not know. I work at their homes. That's all. We have nothing in common. I am speaking about women workers; somewhere they share with us the same lack of respect. If am stressing the respect, it is because the work we do is considered worthless. (Personal interview with Rose, migrant domestic worker from Cameroon, February 2015)

The early 2000s witnessed a growing interest on the part of NGOs in the issue of migrant domestic workers. The Lebanese government was pressured by international human-rights organizations to make adequate reforms in its legislations and policies regarding the working conditions of migrant domestic workers. The adoption of the International Labour Organization Convention No. 189 concerning Decent Work for Domestic Workers in June 2011 put the issue of migrant domestic workers on the global agenda of human rights and further mobilized donors (such as the EU, the Swiss Agency for Development and Cooperation, and UN Women) around this issue. In compliance with this new international agenda, local NGOs started developing projects and programs on migrant domestic workers specifically designed to provide legal, medical, and social assistance in the absence—or because of the absence—of state policies. Again, the NGOs agreed to play the role of the state, exempting it from its responsibilities toward its population by providing these services instead of enhancing mobilization and collective political action. Salameh (2014), Daou (2014), Mitri (2014), and Jad (2004) highlight the rise of more 'managerial' types of organizations, which are less and less action-oriented and more associated with what Wendy Brown (2006) terms "liberal legalism," which seeks to regulate differences in the context of the nation-state. All these elements contribute to the depoliticization of social movements. Depoliticization means that questions of inequality and injustice are perceived as individual and personal rather than political and structural problems: "It involves removing a political phenomenon from comprehension of its *historical* emergence and from the recognition of the *powers* that produce and counter it" (Brown 2006:15).

In the context of migrant domestic workers, this depoliticization occurs first by singling out their experiences as unique or exceptional among working-class experiences and under neoliberalism, an idea that I challenge in chapter 1. The NGOs' projects designed for migrant domestic workers exclusively, for instance, reaffirm the extent to which this issue is understood as separate from the project of securing workers' rights. Second, depoliticization is furthered by following a strategy that gives more importance to legal reform and collaboration with state institutions, such as the Lebanese General Security, as opposed to enhancing the organization and mobilization of domestic workers. The third step is to grant a bigger role to service provision than to the enhancement of collective action. One example is the Consortium on Migrant Domestic Workers, established in 2012 as the result of the growing coordination between NGOs on issues affecting migrant domestic workers. It aims to develop a common data management system that would guarantee an effective referral system for abused migrant domestic workers to the specific organization that provides the needed services, in order to avoid replicating services. In this framework, politics is turned into 'data management' and a 'referral system' of domestic workers, rather than envisioning and creating new labor practices.

Among the NGOs, Kafa is the only Lebanese women's-rights organization that is active on the issue of migrant domestic workers, uncovering the abuse they face, providing services for them, advocating for the abolishment of the *kafala* system, and calling for improvement of their working conditions. However, the dominant approach of the

NGOs, Kafa included, is a humanitarian one, focusing on cases of violence, trafficking, and deaths at the expense of the working conditions of the domestic workers. This approach, which focuses on extreme cases of abuse, constructs migrant domestic workers as helpless victims, rather than political agents under circumscribed conditions. I argue that this framing of migrant domestic workers as victims is the natural consequence of the 'death' of politics, class politics in particular, the growing professionalization of the women's-rights organizations, and the production of women's-rights experts and their beneficiaries.

Class Politics and Contemporary Women's Movements

While women workers' militancy in Lebanon can be traced back to women's industrial actions in nineteenth-century silk factories and in the first half of the twentieth century in the tobacco industry, the problems of working-class women rarely made it to the agenda of the women's-rights activists. Bernadette Daou (2014) distinguishes four waves of women's-rights movements in Lebanon. In conjunction with the independence movement in 1943, the first wave was largely based on the significant participation of women in the national liberation movement. The second wave emerged in the context of the Arab defeat of 1967 against Israel, and the rise of a 'new left.' The third emerged within the context of the post–civil war era, which was marked by a growing trend toward the NGO-ization of women's claims. Finally, the fourth wave was born out of the antiwar and anti-globalization movements in the early 2000s. Despite the relatively long history of the active presence of working-class women in public affairs and in labor activism, the sole form of women's activism that has been recognized in academia, in the press, in women's specialized conferences, and in activism reports is the one led by upper-class women, who rarely challenged the socioeconomic aspect of the patrimonial and patriarchal Lebanese order (Makarem and Rizk 2014).

The early years of the twentieth century were marked by women's literary salons, mainly for upper-class women who also ran charitable organizations, and later women's political unions. The first wave of women activists was predominantly concerned with the anticolonial struggle and the right to vote and to political participation. Its relationship to the poor took place through charity exclusively. The underlying characteristic of this wave was the detachment of women's issues from the domain of the social: "This elite had no awareness of women's needs in other situations, no interest in defending women belonging to lower economic classes, for example . . . the feminist discourse of this generation reflects the degree of overlap between national identity and female identity" (Daou 2014:14–15). The women who emerged from influential families and educated notable classes were interested in the questions of nationalism, colonial rule, and modernization (Abisaab 2010). Parallel to this, women workers and peasants, who at that time constituted more than half of the formal labor force, were at the forefront of the national campaigns against French colonial rule and its monopolization of tobacco production by the Régie. The workers' campaigns were the basis of the political movement for independence that culminated, as Abisaab (2010) notes, in the departure of the French and the promulgation of the labor law in 1946. These campaigns did not stop with the declaration of the independent national state that was regarded as an extension of, rather than a break with, colonialism. The working-class women active in the anticolonial struggle shared little of the national ideals of upper-class women. The following lengthy extract from Abissaab's study questions gender as an independent analytical category that unites women despite class divisions, and captures best the different interests, goals, and aspirations of the women on the opposite sides of class politics:

> It [women workers' activism] was a public activism that was more suspicious of modernization, particularly when mechanization was introduced to industrial manufactures. It was less concerned with promoting women as the keepers and promoters of the moral ideals of "the nation" against European colonialism, than with direct rejection of colonial exploitation of their labor, its severe disruption of the peasant family as a producing unit, and its implementations of new and "modern" forms of patriarchal practices that, on the one hand, removed women from direct family control and, on the other, forced them to accept half a man's wage at the industrial plant. Working women's struggle against the French and the Lebanese colonial state and capitalists was specifically for and about women's place in the market economy and their waged labor. Peasant and

working women always have been in the public and have always worked. Seclusion and segregation were however, what upper-class and educated women writers of this earlier period tried to change in connection with anticolonial struggle and the discourse of modernization. (Abisaab 2010:36)

Abisaab concludes that "there is more than one trajectory of women's history in Syria–Lebanon, and a common gender language or culture of resistance is absent. Beyond rallies against the Régie monopoly and French colonial rule, upper-class feminism and working class feminism rarely met" (2010:36).

In the early 1960s the national question remained the basic preoccupation for the second-wave feminists. These feminists, who became politicized in the union and student movements, were part of a broader struggle for socialism, and for resistance to colonialism and to occupation. The 1970s and the 1980s witnessed the creation of different feminist organizations that constituted sister organizations of the nationalist and leftist political parties. Hence the League of Rights for Lebanese Women (*Lajnat Huquq al-Mar'a*) was a faction of the Communist Party. The Lebanese Democratic Assembly of Women (*al-Tajammo' al-Nisa'i al-Dimoqrati al-Lubnani* (RDFL) was founded as a sister organization of the Organization of Communist Action. The Progressive Women's Union (*al-Itihad al-Nisa'i al-Taqaddomi*) was founded as a sister organization of the Progressive Socialist Party. Despite the fact that some of these organizations, such as the RDFL, addressed the issue of women's rights at work, and hosted awareness-raising sessions for working-class women, these actions remained marginal on their agenda compared to the questions of national independence, relief work, and resistance to Israel. Despite the fact that the claim for recognition of the economic value of domestic work figured as one of the objectives of the RDFL, it never materialized into a public campaign to pressure the government and employers toward this recognition. Daou argues that these feminist organizations had no agenda independent of the political parties to which they were attached—political parties which did not conceive of feminist struggles independent of the struggle for socialism—and that "the victory of the feminist cause depends on the victory of the socialist cause" (Daou 2014:18).

A new wave emerged following the civil war, characterized by the growing NGO-ization of women's issues. The principal event for these third-wave feminists was the Beijing Fourth World Conference on Women in 1995. Within this context, many specialized organizations have emerged, such as the Lebanese Council to Resist Violence against Women (LECORVAW) and the Collective for Research and Training on Development (CRTDA), and later on Kafa (Enough Violence and Exploitation). A new language was born, such as 'positive discrimination' and 'gender-based violence,' parallel to the emergence of 'new' causes. Thus, concludes Daou, "The structures of these new NGOs meet the requirements of international donors: the initiatives are turned into projects, the militants into 'project coordinators,' 'professionals' and 'employees'" (2014:21). The leftist discourse of the 1970s feminists was turned into a single-issue, rights-based discourse on partial reforms; in this sense, "women's liberation was dissociated from the pre-condition of the liberation of the society" (Daou 2014:23). In this context, the majority of women, especially those who belong to the working class, were marginalized from the agenda, politics, and strategies of the women's-rights NGOs (Salameh 2014). A line has been drawn between the professional women's-rights advocates and their 'beneficiaries.' "The latter are often seen in the position of victims rather than women who share the same cause" (Salameh 2014:78). The hierarchal structures of these organizations turn them into exclusive spaces of experts and professionals who strategize, advocate, lobby, and create policies for women, in isolation from the women whom they claim to defend. Salameh argues that these structures alienate working-class women, who "are turned into victims, rather than being part of platforms where women's voices and experiences can be raised and shared" (Salameh 2014:78).

The fourth wave of feminists emerged from within the LGBT movement, born out of the antiwar and anti-globalization demonstrations in 2000. These feminist militants focus on sexual and bodily rights as well as identity politics. Despite the fact that they self-identify as anticapitalist and anticolonial, they are led by educated middle- and upper-middle-class women emerging out of Beirut's most prestigious private universities (Daou 2014).

Lebanese feminist movements throughout their modern history have predominantly sidelined the class dimension. Little interest has been given to the actual lives and experiences of poor and working-class women. Similarly, few women's groups have taken up the cause of women migrant workers. Instead, priority is given to the 'Lebanese woman,' as a prominent feminist activist once put it in a public discussion on migrant domestic workers in 2011. An activist from Kafa observed: "I feel that women's-rights organization continue to resist the idea of handling the cause of migrant domestic workers. They would say: 'Let's find work for the Lebanese women first before the migrants'" (personal interview, January 2015). This lack of support for women migrant workers on the part of the majority of women's groups can be attributed to the national-centric ideology of these groups. The result is a general marginalization of working-class women. In this regard, it is worth observing that the struggle of migrant domestic workers, which has received increasing attention from international human-rights organizations, has received no support from most of the women's-rights groups except Kafa (and Nasawiya before its dissolution in 2014). This marginalization can be attributed to the fact that each organization is 'specialized' in a 'single-issue' or specific mandate. But most importantly, the predominantly middle-class women who make up these organizations have not acknowledged the role they also play in denying these workers their rights (Ng 2004). In other words, there would be a conflict of interest in claiming, for instance, a minimum wage for domestic workers, since such a measure would work against the members' own economic interests.

The attention that migrant domestic workers have received, especially from Kafa, did not come out of concern with working-class women in general, but mostly, as mentioned earlier, followed the international mobilization of funds intended to assist this category of women specifically. In Kafa's framework the issue of migrant domestic workers is a question of violence against women rather than labor exploitation.

Violence against Women or Labor Rights?

Kafa, a prominent women's-rights advocacy organization, was founded in 2005 with the mission of combating violence against women. It officially began working on the question of migrant domestic workers in 2010 as part of its anti-trafficking program. One Kafa coordinator explains how they frame the question of migrant domestic workers.

— *We wanted to address this issue from the perspective of gender-based violence, not from the labor and poverty perspective. We are facing problems in propagating the problem from a gendered perspective because the dominant framework is the one related to labor rights and workers' migration. But we must not forget that they are women, and they constitute one of the largest female labor forces in the country. From here, the violence exercised against the domestic worker within the household is not dissociated from the violence exercised by the husband against his wife. The power dynamics within the family are replicated against the domestic worker, even though in most cases the source of physical and psychological violence against the domestic worker is the woman.*

— *Do you mean that the violence against the domestic worker is linked to domestic violence?*

— *It's not linked to domestic violence. But we can say that if the Lebanese woman is battered within the family, most probably the domestic worker is battered too, either by the male perpetrator of violence or by the female victim of violence. What I mean is that the power dynamic between the husband and the wife is the same between the employer, man or woman, and the domestic worker. It's violence. This is what we want to get to. It's violence that is practiced against the domestic worker because she's a woman. Of course, because she's a woman, from a different race, color, religion, and poorer . . . but we cannot forget her gender identity.* (Personal interview with Kafa coordinator, January 2015)

The gender-specific approach of Kafa to domestic work is a continuation of the work of Kafa against domestic violence. This approach addresses the difficult working conditions, including physical and psychological violence that female and male employers direct against their women domestic workers. However, a study conducted by Ray Jureidini shows that there is no significant correlation between abuse of the domestic worker and abuse of the female employer by her husband (2011a:9). Violence between employers and employees is enhanced by the *kafala* system that renders the migrant domestic worker dependent on the goodwill of her employers. The framing of domestic workers' issues as gendered violence thus leads to the questioning of the sponsorship system. However, in this framework, the labor dimension is sidelined. The concern that is being neglected is that the economic value of this labor is not recognized because it is considered an extension of the natural role of women and part of the informal economy.

The neglect of the labor element in Kafa's framework relegates the discussion about labor rights and the social organization of reproductive labor to a secondary position. The gender-based-violence approach to domestic workers, despite its importance in integrating the gendered and racialized exploitation of workers by their employers with spousal violence, is not successful in negotiating the differences between labor organizing and domestic violence work. The latter is largely based on institutionalized responses to domestic violence, where survivors are turned into clients and activists into service providers.

In fact, in 2013 Kafa started to organize a group of Nepali domestic workers (the NARI group), with the support of the General Federation of Nepalese Trade Unions and Anti-Slavery International. Organizing the Nepalese over national lines is an act that mimics the pattern of migrant community organizing, a problem that the union for the domestic workers is trying to overcome. This pattern is a spontaneous form of organizing in which migrants meet over common language, culture, and religion. The community in that sense is a bridge between spontaneous community formation and the more open political form of organizing such as the union. However, while the NARI group was initiated by Kafa following a top-down style of organizing, other migrant communities have self-organized historically, even before the intervention of the NGOs on their behalf. The Nepalese workers are among the least organized because they are smaller in numbers and among the most recent migrant workers in the country. The management of this community organizing is overdetermined by Kafa in everything related to funding events, training, and advocacy work. Kafa's motivation to organize NARI, as one Kafa coordinator puts it, "is to empower a group that becomes a reference whenever a worker is in trouble or is abused." In that sense, NARI plays only a limited role as an intermediary between the abused worker and the NGO, or as a referral system that links the worker in need of assistance to the service provider. This approach limits the political potential of mobilization for domestic workers and also confines them in the category of victims of violence. The labor approach for domestic workers, on the contrary, opens up another aspect for mobilizing, one that is based on the shared experience of exploitation of labor and working-class solidarity among women across nationality and race.

Toward the Revaluation of Domestic Labor

Women's-rights activists in Lebanon rarely discuss the mixed pattern of work that women workers undertake outside and inside the house. When the labor rights of women workers are raised, such as the right to social security and equal pay and so forth, these demands are not linked to the women workers' conditions within the family. Official labor statistics claim that women constitute 23 percent of the labor force in Lebanon (Salameh 2014); other sources estimate that women represent 35 percent of the total number of employed workers (Khalaf 2002). These figures exclude the informal sector and imply that the majority of women in Lebanon do not work. In other words, the labor of women performed informally or in the household is made invisible and officially unrecognized. Rima (name has been changed), a feminist militant, says:

Domestic work is a problematic that can unite Lebanese and migrant working-class women. However, the feminist activists either talked about women's social reproduction role inside the house, or about women workers' rights outside the house. They never made the link between the two spheres; they never spoke about the woman as a worker both inside and outside the domestic sphere. However, as a feminist I don't accept that my liberation from domestic work takes place at the expense of the liberation of another woman. Many Lebanese women consider that they are liberated because they work outside the house, while they employ a domestic worker very cheaply. I see that the societal and economic revaluing of domestic work is a struggle that should unite women. Lebanese women should know that the wage they pay for the domestic worker reflects the worth they themselves attach to this labor. This means it reflects the value they attribute to their own labor. (Personal interview, January 2015)

Rima makes an important point that is missing in the discourse of Kafa and women's-rights organizations in general, which is the idea that the struggle for the labor rights of domestic workers will open up the political possibility of the recognition of domestic work as 'real' work, whoever is performing it, whether a full-time Lebanese housewife or a migrant worker. As Salameh eloquently puts it: "The non-recognition of women's domestic work as an economic value and the exploitation of migrant domestic workers relieves the state from the burden of providing those services, placing them on the backs of women" (Salameh 2014:72). The non-recognition of the economic value of women's domestic labor runs parallel to the societal and official celebration of women as caregivers and housewives. Given the fact that the private family is responsible for the well-being of its members in the absence of adequate state policies in that field, it is the women who carry the burden of the unpaid caregiving services for children, the elderly, and persons with special needs within the family. Hence, the labor-related framing of domestic workers allows for a discussion on welfare policies for the household, such as state-funded childcare policies, care for the elderly and disabled, and income for domestic work, which are still absent from public discussions and the agendas of women's-rights groups. Yet the common struggle for the re-valuing of domestic work should not at the same time subordinate differences of race and nationality that structure the encounter between non-migrant and migrant women. Gutierrez-Rodríguez argues in the context of Europe:

> *Though these two women might share the effects of structural violence against women, the exploitative effects of the logic of capital accumulation and heteronormativity, these moments are crossed by the logic of the coloniality of power. Thus, while these women might, for example, share the same nasty feeling of "disgust" attached to the social devaluation of domestic work, this feeling is connoted by different moments of domination. . . . Political organizing around the question of feminization of labor, thus, demands more than a retrieval of identity politics as the fabric of the feminization of labor is embedded in the coloniality of labor.* (Gutierrez-Rodríguez, 2010:159)

Indeed, the non-recognition of the value of domestic work is not the result of its feminization only, but also of its growing racialization. In his study on the history of migrant domestic workers in Lebanon, Jureidini (2009) notes that prior to the civil war, Palestinian women from

Lebanon's refugee camps, Kurdish refugees, and women from neighboring Arab countries, such as Syria and Egypt, constituted the majority of the domestic labor force. With the beginning of the Lebanese civil war in 1975, Arab domestic workers were slowly replaced by women of African and Asian origins. In the postwar environment in Lebanon, there has been a pronounced internationalization of the domestic labor force. Hence, any labor approach to domestic work must critically confront racist and nationalist discourses in the struggle against exploitation of migrant workers and migratory policies at large. In fact, the plight of migrant domestic workers in Lebanon is not just a legal issue that can be remedied by reforming the *kafala* system. It reflects deeper class, racial, and gendered prejudices that must be addressed. Domestic workers' oppression is threefold: they are working-class women of color from the global south. In this regard, coloniality of power is inflicted with gendered and class divisions. In this framework, the labor unions must recognize the insufficiency of interpretations based on class as a universal entity. Likewise, the feminist interpretations of paid domestic work are insufficient when they do not incorporate the elements of class and race.

The Perfectly Tailored Victim and Its Binary Other

> *Kafa helps mistreated, abused, and raped women, but I am not in this condition and I don't personally suffer from these problems. Kafa also deals on a case-by-case basis, not with domestic workers only, but with all women. But the trade union is something different. It's us who are trying to unite to defend our rights, in our name. This is the difference. There are many NGOs who help and protect us, but following their own terms. But in order to eradicate the roots of the problem, to assert our own rights, we cannot wait for someone to lead the struggle on our behalf. It depends on us and us only, as domestic workers. The NGOs help us in each case that appears. However, what we want from this trade union is to eradicate the roots of our exploitation.* (Personal interview with Lily, domestic worker from Madagascar, January 2015)

Lily acknowledges the importance of the services provided by Kafa. However, she expresses her lack of feeling of ownership within the

NGO in contrast to the trade union, which she considers as a place that unites workers to defend their rights "in our name." What Lily is expressing here is the need for NGOs to be supportive of the workers' struggle without dictating the terms of this struggle. She also expresses her frustration with the category of 'abused woman' into which she must fit in order to benefit from the services offered by Kafa. She notes the discrepancy between her personal experience as worker and this categorization. Her insistence on her subject positioning as 'domestic worker' challenges the identity of 'mistreated, abused, and raped' woman assumed by Kafa. Gemma from the Philippines shares similar concerns.

The role of the NGOs is helping us. But their help has limits. They say: 'This is the allotted amount for this project, for example, and when the funds are short, that's it! We stop at that.' While for us, having our union is the sacrifice we make. It's the commitment in our heart. We are the key actors and players in that union. It's not you. It's not the ILO. It's us. (Personal interview with Gemma, domestic worker from the Philippines, February 2015)

The ways in which Gemma and Lily define themselves and their fellow workers constitute a shared understanding that begins to take shape in the union organization process. The statements put forward by these workers challenge the framework upheld by the NGOs that tend to manage them as victims.

A study conducted by Kafa entitled "Dreams for Sale: The Exploitation of Domestic Workers from Recruitment in Nepal and Bangladesh to Working in Lebanon" (2014) found that the migrant is first a victim who has been deceived by recruiting agents and brokers in her country of origin. Second, the migrant becomes a victim of forced labor upon her arrival in Lebanon. Third, the migrant domestic worker is a victim of emotional, physical, and sexual violence exercised by the employers or the placement agencies. In this account Kafa has drawn the image of the perfect victim: a domestic worker who has been deceived, abused, and exploited throughout her migration trajectory. In this portrayal of extreme victimhood, replete with images of slavery, a depressing and potentially disempowering scenario is being constructed. While the victimhood discourse can be useful in propagating and rendering visible the dire conditions of the migrant domestic workers within a human-rights framework, it constructs the domestic worker as an incapacitated subject who cannot be an active actor in transforming her reality, but who, on the contrary, needs someone to make the change on her behalf. After all, advocacy work necessitates a language of victims to demonstrate the large number of people affected negatively by a certain policy. This framework cannot possibly reflect the daily struggle of the domestic workers, how they sustain themselves under this regime and in certain cases become militants for workers' rights. In fact, the day-to-day lives and resistance of the women go unnoticed and invisible to the state, the law, the NGOs, and the research community in general. Gemma reacts to this victimhood discourse put forward by the NGOs.

I am not afraid. I always say to my colleagues: FEAR has two meanings. The first is: Forget Everything And Run. The second: Face Everything And Rise. This is what I share with them. If the fear will control your life, until when you will hold it? I know, it will take months, maybe years for the government to approve what we are doing, but we keep on fighting. Nothing can stop us now. The pride that we had last Sunday, nobody can erase it. We made history. Decades will pass. But it will be marked that this generation of workers formed a union on January 25, 2015. You cannot remove this from the record.

Individuation of Rights and Security Concerns

Kafa developed its project on domestic workers to assist victims of violence, providing legal counseling services, psychotherapy, and referral to a temporary safe house for abused domestic workers. The domestic workers who benefit from these services need to meet certain criteria, mainly exposure to sexual and/or physical abuse by employers or the placement agencies' personnel. These services redress individual violations, but they fail to question the structural problems that enable these violations to occur. As Wendy Brown puts it:

While rights may attenuate the subordination and violation to which women are vulnerable in a masculinist social, political, and economic regime, they vanquish neither the regime nor its mechanism of reproduction. (Brown 2000:231)

The rights discourse is limited by the law and the state institutions. For instance, Kafa held an *ad hoc* agreement with the General Security to stop the detention and the deportation of a runaway domestic worker who escaped abuse and approached Kafa for help. The domestic worker in this position was referred to a shelter, which serves as a 'more humane' alternative to the General Security prison. The coordination with the General Security, while it can benefit the domestic worker on an individual basis, allowing her to avoid the insecure fate of deportation or the dire life of being incarcerated for an undefined period in an underground General Security prison, is problematic on a political level. In fact, illegal migrants who are detained by the General Security are usually sentenced to prison, fined, and ultimately face deportation (Human Rights Watch 2008:2). Kafa's coordination with the General Security, however, does not question this apparatus, its long-standing history of violation of migrant workers' and refugees' rights, or its responsibility in oppressing migrants on the basis that they constitute a security threat. Dealing with migrants from a security perspective, as Aradau (2008) has successfully argued, is the first step in the process of rendering them unequal and reducing them to a shadowy existence. In that sense, security acts as a negation to policies that resist discrimination. For example, in January 2014 the General Security issued a directive under which it is permitted to expel migrant workers with children on the grounds that they have started a family in Lebanon. By May of that year, dozens of women migrant workers were deported with their children in a clear violation of the International Covenant on Civil and Political Rights, the Convention on the Elimination of All Forms of Racial Discrimination, and the Convention on the Rights of the Child (Human Rights Watch 2014). Deportation should be seen as a disciplinary practice that acts to regulate the population and which cannot be understood in isolation from the regime of citizenship. In fact, citizenship acts as a marker of identification that regulates the division of humanity into distinct national populations and puts them under different regimes of governance following racial, gendered, and class lines. It is under this regime that the migrant is considered an "excessive subject" recognized only as an anomaly, as someone who "should not be there" (Aradau 2008:191).

It is worth mentioning that such campaigns that seek collaboration with state institutions such as the General Security attract donor organizations that do not, or cannot, question these institutions' records of human-rights violations. For example, in partnership with the Internal Security Forces (ISF), and despite the fact that police forces are famous for their human-rights abuses,[1] Kafa launched sixteen days of activism against violence against women on November 25, 2013, on the occasion of the International Day for the Elimination of Violence against Women, under the title "We Have a Mission: If You're Threatened, Do Not Hesitate to Call 112." The campaign aimed at "rebuilding trust between women victims of violence and the ISF, and informing the public on the ISF's ongoing preparations to provide women with the protection they need" (Kafa 2013). The campaign is part of a wider project implemented by Kafa and the ISF, called "The Role of the Internal Security Forces in Combating Family Violence." This campaign was funded by the United Nations Population Fund, the Italian Embassy in Lebanon, the Norwegian Embassy in Lebanon, the Swedish organization Kvinna Till Kvinna, the Norwegian Popular Aid, Oxfam, Save the Children, and the European Union.

Such campaigns pose critical questions regarding the role of donors in maintaining the status quo and shaping the discourse and strategies of women's organizations (Salameh 2014) and the extent to which these organizations become part and parcel of the regime of governance. Most importantly, as labor activists have stated, coordination with an oppressive state apparatus threatens any initiatives taken by migrant workers to collectively organize. It is legitimate to ask: Will the NGO take a position in support of the trade union for domestic workers, for instance, if the General Security decides to attack the union militants, to incarcerate and deport them? Won't their trade-union militancy jeopardize the relationships that the NGO sustains with the General Security, and consequently risk the operation of their projects, programs, and services?

These relationships between NGOs and the General Security are still unfolding, yet all the indicators suggest that militant unionists for domestic workers will not find support if and when their actions start

---

1   S. Dockery, "HRW: World Should Act on Lebanon Police Abuse," *The Daily Star*, June 27, 2013, http://www.dailystar.com.lb/News/Local-News/2013/Jun-27/221723-hrw-world-should-act-on-lebanon-police-abuse.ashx

to go beyond the accepted norms. An activist at the Migrant Community Center told me, for example, that Caritas-Lebanon, a prominent NGO working on migrant domestic workers' issues, refused to cosign a statement that criticized the General Security and expressed its objection to any confrontation with the state or this institution that might threaten their programs. In fact, Caritas's work is based on a close and cooperative relationship with the General Security in dealing with the problems of migrant domestic workers. Between 2000 and 2001, for instance, Caritas contributed to the funding of the General Security Detention Center in Adliyeh, which is designed specifically for migrants with visa violations. This "controversial agreement" with the General Security allowed Caritas to provide medical and health services in the detention center and to monitor the treatment of the detained migrants (Jureidini 2011b). However, the discourse of the migrant labor activists, such as Lily and Gemma, already challenges the boundaries of the hegemonic model of activism set by the NGOs. For them, their trade union will enhance their collective rights as domestic workers. They portray the individual problems of abuse that face domestic workers as structural ones, and they conceive their struggle as a collective and historical one.

Conclusion

This chapter questions the class-biased politics of the women's-rights agenda. It argues in favor of an alternative feminist politics that seeks to advance gender and class justice for women irrespective of nationality and race. It also argues in favor of a politics of labor that opens up the space for collective action as part of an emancipatory project and moves out of the restricted terrain of identity politics and narratives of victimhood. In my fieldwork, migrant domestic workers repeated on many instances that "we are workers with rights." Despite the fact that such a call does not constitute a break from capitalism, but occurs within it, and hence remains partial, it still represents an emancipatory move from the regime of governance and the securitizing practices that categorize migrants as threat, other, and excess.

The problem with the politics adopted by women's-rights organizations depicts a larger problem related to the growing institutionalization, professionalization, and depoliticization of the women's movement, where claims for justice for women are turned into data management and referral systems. Contemporary Lebanese women's-rights organizations resort to a liberal discourse on rights calling for state intervention through its regulatory system. This is largely the effect of the demise of class politics and the critique of capitalism and its culture. In this framework, claims concerned with gender and race (as in the case of rights for migrant domestic workers) appear not as supplement for class politics but as external to them. I give one example that further clarifies my argument: in a discussion with one Kafa coordinator, I was told that class is a variable that acts as a layer of exploitation of migrant domestic workers next to race and gender. In this framework, class is recognized and named, but not theorized or developed as a domain for social identification or as an axis of mobilization. In other words, the 'death of politics' gave rise to women's-rights organizations that address migrant domestic workers' issues separately and as part of heavily funded campaigns and projects. This depoliticization of the women's-rights movement is extended even further by donor funding preferences for 'empowerment' and 'capacity building,' requiring measurable changes in women's lives, instead of feminist consciousness and grassroots organizing. This has reconfigured feminist and women's politics on the national level. Movement-building and agitational politics were replaced with training expert reports, funded short-term programs of empowerment, and advocacy campaigns. As Manicom puts it, "the danger is that the objectives of women's emancipation are buried by the rationalities of administration" (2001:11). Indeed, the victimhood discourse can be understood as a consequence for these "rationalities of administration" that turn the migrant domestic worker into an object of power for the NGOs and the state. In this discourse, a line is drawn between 'us,' the women's-rights defenders, and 'them,' the victims whom the women's-rights campaigners design projects to save or call on the state to save. This construction neglects the everyday array of mechanisms employed by these workers to cope, to negotiate, and even to resist their precarious conditions. But more importantly, "a politics that rests on narratives of victimization does not inspire solidarity."[2]

---

2 S. Carlson, "Mapping a New Economy: The Geographer David Harvey Says Fixing Inequality Will Take More than Tinkering," *The Chronicle Review*, May 12, 2014. http://chronicle.com/article/Mapping-a-New-Economy/146433

In this context the domestic workers in Lebanon started to organize and mobilize following a union model, pumping new blood into the veins of the trade-union movement in the country. Their actions take place within a framework of insecurity resulting from the regimes of governance that manage them as aliens with no or limited rights. Their work reminds us of the fact that power and resistance inhabit the same moment, where "no matter how terrifying a given system may be, there always remain the possibilities of resistance, disobedience, and oppositional groupings" (Foucault, cited in Brown 2009:397). This contradictory act of power is what is largely missing from the theorization of women's groups, who tend to inscribe their 'beneficiaries' under the one category of 'victims.'

CHAPTER 4

Women Domestic Workers and Trade-Union Organizing: Challenges and Possibilities

On January 25, 2015, domestic workers started to gather at the wedding hall facing FENASOL's headquarters in Cola in Beirut. Welcoming signs in different languages were hung at the front door. At 10 am the hall was completely full, with over 300 workers all wearing red clothes to project a sense of steadfastness and organization. A common feeling was shared by the workers; starting today, they would be "making history," a sentence that I heard repeated by many workers with a noticeable sense of pride. Indeed, this day was a historic day for them as they declared the founding of their trade union, the first of its kind in Lebanon and in the Arab region. The pride the workers manifested and the sense of 'making history' they expressed emanated largely from their conception that what they are doing represents a challenge to the norm, to authority, to the law, and to the representation of domestic workers as helpless victims. They did not wait for the state to give its approval; they did it themselves, launching their union irrespective of the government's opinion. Their pride was rooted in the power they felt emanating from their collectiveness on that day, to claim their rights in an occupation that isolates workers and individualizes their problems. Over 300 workers from Ethiopia, Nepal, Sri Lanka, Sudan, the Philippines, Lebanon, Madagascar, South Africa, Bangladesh, and Senegal held their congress under the slogan: "The Right to Organize on the Basis of Decent Work and the Path toward Achieving Social Justice." Their congress marked the first real workers' congress in Lebanon since the 1980s, in which workers deliberated freely and democratically. It originated from a precarious labor category that has been historically sidelined from formal labor unions: domestic workers, who are predominantly women and migrants. The importance of their actions rests, however, on the fact that it came at a particular moment of general mistrust in labor unions to lead change, and at a time where the working class has lost its organizational instruments, while the majority of Lebanese workers and their migrant counterparts remain outside organizers' reach. The actions of the domestic workers restored the hope that organizing the unorganized is still a possibility; more than a possibility, it is a necessity under the current neoliberal regime.

This chapter examines the process of organizing migrant domestic workers and their union. The organization offers complex and different positions of power and influence. The complexity pertains to the fact that power is not a thing that can easily be seized, but a system of relations within which the actors circulate (Agrikoliansky, in Fillieule, Mathieu, and Péchu 2009). Analyzing the plurality of positions of power invites, in addition and more importantly, an analysis of the structures, leadership, and nature of the discourses that this attempt at unionization seeks to mobilize. The purpose of this chapter is to explore the relations of power and relative privilege within a space that brings together workers from different national backgrounds, which is marked by racial and gendered relations, to look at the emerging potentialities, as well as the obstacles confronting this new organizational experience.

Workers and Individualized Services

Sunday, December 28, is a rainy day in Beirut. On this morning, the streets are still almost empty of cars and residents. It took me only 20 minutes on my scooter to get from Mansourieh, in the Matn district of Mount Lebanon Governorate, to the West Beirut Cola area where FENASOL is located. My plan was to attend one of the meetings for domestic workers, who were gathering every Sunday, in a long learning and organizing process that lasted for 18 months at FENASOL with the support of the ILO bureau in Beirut and other NGOs. I reached Cola at 10 am. Usually this area is very busy, as it is one of the most important transportation hubs in the city and is also home to universities, mosques, markets, and shops offering fast food and cheap merchandise. Drivers and passengers come from the four corners of the city, forming a mix of

Lebanese workers and students, Syrians, and Palestinians. They converge at the square to move to other neighborhoods in Beirut, the suburbs, and other parts of Lebanon in the south, the north, and Bekaa. A bridge that divides the area constitutes a temporary shelter for many homeless people, Lebanese and Syrians, whose numbers fluctuate depending on police and gang raids. The area took its name from the Coca-Cola factory that disappeared a few decades ago and was replaced by a parking lot. During the civil war, Cola and the neighboring areas, such as Wata al-Musaytbeh, witnessed the proliferation of leftist parties, including the Communist Party, that established their headquarters in the area, in addition to trade unions. FENASOL established its headquarters here in 1976. Because of its easy access and the socioeconomic composition of its residents, the area is strategic for trade-union activities.

On my arrival at FENASOL's headquarters, I saw that the Federation's center, which I used to visit often before my travel to Egypt in 2012 and was always almost empty but for a handful of Lebanese workers who occasionally come for specific services, is now almost full with dozens of migrant domestic workers, either to ask questions about how to join the union or to complain to Castro Abdallah, FENASOL's president, about individual problems. Suzanne, a Malagasy domestic worker, came that morning with five new migrant workers who wanted to join the union. One of them is Sanjip, an Indian man from Punjab, who has been in Lebanon for 30 years and who overstayed his residency following the death of his sponsor and the closing of the sewing shop where he used to work. He came with the hope that the trade union would help him legalize his residency in Lebanon. In fact, many workers believe that the union's goal is to solve their immediate problems, such as residency and work permits, which is what brings them here. Abdallah, who meets with the workers in his office, takes notes of the complaints, and either resolves them directly or simply asks the worker to return a few days later. His attention to every case that he hears creates a sense of trust with the migrant domestic workers. Resolving day-to-day problems of the workers, although it requires much effort and time, especially for a federation that lacks resources, volunteers, and personnel, is an important strategy for engaging with the domestic workers.

The process of organizing domestic workers occurred at a slow pace, compared to the usual process for more standardized forms of work.

There are, in fact, many obstacles to organizing these workers: "isolated, dispersed, and difficult to reach, these are working lives beyond the scope of conventional modes of labor organizing" (Cornwall 2013: viii). Despite this difficulty, migrant domestic workers started to join as the news about their trade union began to circulate among migrant workers' communities and networks by word of mouth, and the union now numbers 350 members.

Despite the importance of FENASOL's interventions in everyday problems on behalf of domestic workers, there is the risk of creating a 'new NGO,' to the extent that FENASOL turns into another center for providing individual services for workers despite its trade-union organizing and focus on collective bargaining. This challenge is a real one, especially within the context of the already weakened trade-union movement in the country and the transformation of the labor unions into bureaucratic bodies, which resolve grievances arising between workers and employers rather than organizing workers and engaging in workplace agitation.

FENASOL and UN Funding

During my interviews with FENASOL's leadership, I was constantly told that what had hindered the Federation from extending its base to set up and support workers' unions, especially in the informal sector, is its lack of financial resources. It was only when the ILO approached FENASOL in 2012 with a project to organize migrant domestic workers, offering funds and practical support such as consultancies and training, that FENASOL's leadership decided to embark on this project. In one exchange with the coordinator of a local NGO that deals with migrant domestic workers, I found out that a few years earlier she had approached several trade unions to discuss the issue of unionizing domestic workers, but they showed no interest.

The reliance on UN funding, as in the case of the ILO, is a clear demonstration of the extent to which labor unions have become dissociated from the workers, weak and irrelevant in influencing social and economic policies. However, this cooperation offers advantages as well as disadvantages. On one level, it allows the Federation to forge international networks and helps it develop transnational alliances on labor rights. It also secures financial resources for the Federation, allowing it to reach a broader section of workers locally. On the other hand, reliance on external funding risks the co-option of labor unions by global governance, as has happened with other social movements such as the women's-rights movements (Daou 2014). It can also jeopardize the political independence, as well as the goals, of labor unions. There is the further risk that the Federation's easy access to UN funding might steer it away from worker outreach and organizing and in the direction of developing funded projects, which treat workers as service beneficiaries rather than union militants.

The organizing of domestic workers was initiated by the ILO, beginning with Participatory Action Research (PAR) conducted between May 2012 and December 2014. In a regional 'tripartite' conference held in Cairo in 2012 on ILO Convention No. 189, entitled "Raising Awareness and Sharing Knowledge on Decent Work for Domestic Workers," the ILO, in the presence of state representatives, pushed the idea of organizing domestic workers in Arab countries as a precondition for the ratification of the Convention. For that purpose and during the same year, the ILO proposed to implement a PAR in Lebanon with the objective of organizing domestic workers, raising awareness about their rights guaranteed by the Convention, building synergies among the workers, NGOs, and unions, and increasing the representation of migrant domestic workers in ILO activities and in NGO and union advocacy campaigns in Lebanon. At that time, the ILO was still looking for a potential labor federation ally to implement the project; the choice fell on FENASOL because it was the only federation that agreed to cooperate. As one ILO official says, "The CGTL still considers the domestic workers as servants unworthy of labor rights." A CGTL employee further explains the position held by the CGTL's leadership regarding migrant domestic workers. He says, "Ghassan Ghosson [the president of the CGTL] told me during a private discussion on the margin of a regional meeting on migrant domestic workers to which the CGTL was invited: 'Do you really want me to equate my servant with the Lebanese worker regarding wages and rights?!'" That year, FENASOL decided to withdraw its membership from the CGTL and announced that it will invest its efforts in creating an alternative democratic and independent workers' center. Organizing migrant domestic workers was an expression of FENASOL's commitment in that regard. But it is also driven by the hostility between the CGTL and

FENASOL's leadership and the latter's quest for an official recognition of its federation as a representative of workers in Lebanon, which would grant FENASOL a status of interlocutor with the government on an equal footing with the CGTL in all issues pertaining to social and economic policies and tripartite negotiations. Unionizing the domestic workers is also a contested project, not only vis-à-vis the CGTL, but also within FENASOL, because some of the affiliated Lebanese union leaders do not perceive the project as a priority at a moment when the majority of native Lebanese workers are not unionized either.

The implementation of the PAR took place in collaboration with migrant community leaders, NGOs, and FENASOL. Initially the project was driven by the ILO and the NGOs, with FENASOL offering its Cola headquarters as a meeting space. The language of the PAR organizers is largely based on NGO terminologies such as 'capacity building' and 'advocacy.' As an example, the aim of one of the PAR sessions was the following:

> *All research participants (research team and domestic workers) will identify needed normative and advocacy interventions to address the problems identified. ILO will provide much of the normative insights, NGOs will advise on effective advocacy techniques (online activism, poster campaigns, street mobs . . .), and FENASOL will formulate the action plan using union-related terminology.* (Email addressed to PAR NGOs participants, February 13, 2013)

Eventually the PAR led to the creation of the founding committee for the domestic workers' union.

Forging Workers' Collective Identity

Essential to trade-union organizing and to the effectiveness of collective action is the extent to which members share a sense of common identity and interests. Given the social isolation, diverse nationalities, and conditions in which the migrant domestic workers operate, shared class interests cannot just be automatically assumed, but have to be built. This process of collectivizing the identity has historically taken place in other settings through community organizing, in which common language, religious affiliation, and national belonging constituted a pull around which the migrant workers organized. In contrast, the union for domestic workers needs to overcome nationality and religious lines and organize around common labor experiences. Among the domestic workers' members, a core group of around 30 workers were engaged in the process in its formative stage and acted as the main advocates and mobilizers among their respective communities.

The organizers were well aware of the diverse constituency of the union's members, especially in terms of nationality. The resulting focus on livelihood and common experiences of exploitation, lack of social and formal recognition of the value of domestic work, and its exemption from legislation regulating workers in the formal sectors, all reveal a form of labor politics that seeks to forge an understanding of shared working experiences of domestic work. These concerns acted as a gravitational pull necessary to bring the workers together.

The workers took part in all the stages of the research and learned about each other's experiences in the process. In this way, the labor experiences of individuals began to be forged into a collective whole. The insights generated through the PAR were then discussed in common meetings attended by workers from all the nationalities. These meetings were essential in creating a sense of commonality among workers and allowing them to see the structural patterns of their exploitation represented by the *kafala* system, the recruiting agencies, the laws, and the migration policies. In these meetings, they found out that the problems they faced, as domestic workers from a particular nationality, were not exclusive to them, but also shared by workers from other nationalities. Gemma's words express the importance the workers accorded to these meetings in forging their collective identity as workers.

Every meeting we had with the different communities, I wanted to make sure that we stressed the idea of solidarity. Now we don't say Philippines, Sri Lanka, Ethiopia, and Bangladesh. We say we are the unionists. We are the women workers. We don't mention communities. We emphasize women working together. That's how we have succeeded in having a union. I always take out my union identity card and I raise it with my hand and ask: "Who has this?" In response, the members would wave their cards. I say: "You have this card now. If someone looks at you in different ways here, you say: 'Hey! I am one of you!'" This is always what I emphasize. We are all domestic workers. (Personal interview with Gemma, union executive board member from the Philippines, January 2015)

Rose from Cameroon also addresses the collective identity emanating from the union, which she perceives as a way to obtain respect and make domestic workers visible.

All domestic workers have the same problems. If we have a union today, it is because we sat down together, we raised questions, and we finally came to the conclusion that all domestic workers have the same problems, whatever their nationality. We have the same problems and we live the same silence. That is why the union for me and for other women is a way to shout out loud and say that we exist. Grant us the respect we deserve. (Personal interview with Rose, domestic worker from Cameroon, February 2015)

The PAR was coupled with training programs offered by ILO and the NGOs, which helped close the gaps in workers' knowledge about their rights. The training focused on the meaning and purposes of trade unions, on how to campaign and strategize, on the economic value of domestic labor, on the problems with the *kafala* system, and on the labor law.

Besides the fact that union training and research offered a space for a collective worker identity to emerge, the workers had a variety of other motivations for joining the union. For some, as mentioned above, it meant a place where they can receive support for their immediate problems. For others, forming a union meant creating a space where they can forge solidarity, enhance mutual support, and bargain collectively for their rights with the government and employers. As Lily puts it:

Why is this union important for me? If I am alone I cannot face my employer with my request to have a day off to rest or to sleep. She [the employer] will not be convinced that Sundays are indeed important for us, because it's the day we come together as domestic workers, eat together, and recharge our energy to cope with the week. On our own, we cannot claim that. Thanks to this union we can pressure now collectively for our right, we can fight together, and prove that we exist, that we are citizens, like all citizens, we are not properties of our employers. (Personal interview with Lily, union member from Madagascar, January 2015)

When I asked Mala from Sri Lanka what the union means to her, she replied:

I have been working and working for 33 years now, nonstop, and a few years from now I will have to go back to Sri Lanka and say good-bye to Lebanon. I will return to Sri Lanka in my old age, and I don't know what I have there. I spent money on my children. I spent money on making a house there. What I want to make through this union is a project that guarantees for the women something for when they retire and go back home. Something like a deposit so that when they get sick, they can use it. For 33 years, I have been paying money for insurance companies. Now there's nothing for me in Sri Lanka. We should think about our own lives. (Personal interview with Mala, union executive board member, February 2015)

Mala, or Malani, arrived in Lebanon 33 years ago. She was told that she was going to work in Cyprus. Trafficked by boat, she found herself in the middle of civil-war-tormented Beirut. She left behind four children in Sri Lanka who were able to complete their university degrees and get married, thanks to her remittances. Mala has spent most of her life in Lebanon. She knows Beirut, its neighborhoods, its churches, and its NGOs better than she knows her home town. During her life in Lebanon, she forged connections among her Sri Lankan community and she ultimately became the community leader. Today Mala is 62 years old; she feels too old for her job. She is tired and wants to retire. However, she is not allowed the option of retiring in Lebanon, because the right to family reunification and citizenship is denied to her as 'unskilled' labor. In fact, according to Lebanese residency regulations, certain categories of low-wage workers, including domestic workers, are not allowed to sponsor residency for their spouses and children. After more than three decades of working "nonstop," Mala is faced with the fact that she has to think about how to relocate to Sri Lanka and what her life will look like in her home country.

Mala's example shows the ways in which the personal histories, trajectories, gender, age, class, and race shape women workers' political subjectivities and practices. In that sense, Mala attaches a different meaning to the union. The union, for her, is not only about solving immediate problems that surface while they are on the job as migrant domestic workers, but problems that will face them when they leave their work and ultimately retire. While younger workers' political militancy is turned to the present, the older ones are turned to the future.

The Paradox of Leadership

Those who play a leading position within the union for domestic workers are migrant women who have been in the country between seven and 30 years. As freelance domestic workers (which means that they have made an arrangement with their *kafil* so that he/she keeps sponsoring them while they work and live outside his/her house), their labor experiences are also different from the majority of migrant domestic workers in secluded households. The longer they have been in Lebanon and with their employers, the more they are able to establish relations based on trust with their employers and thus enjoy greater freedom of mobility in comparison to their newly arrived colleagues. These women are also older than the other members. Age is an important factor in leadership; it gives the women symbolic power as the most knowledgeable and helps them gain the respect of their community members. Rose from Cameroon says, "I became a leader of the community because my compatriots chose me. I think they made this choice based on the fact that I have been in Lebanon for a long time, that I am older, and because I try to bring support for them even on the moral level."

Gemma has a somewhat special relationship with her employer. She has worked for the same woman employer for over 17 years, during which a relation based on trust was forged which allowed her freedom of mobility. Gemma became friends with her employer, the two women having a lot in common as single mothers who had to face life on their own. She says: "She knows me very well. She is divorced and she supports her children. At the time of my arrival she was also depressed, and since we were able to communicate we became friends. We talked and we understood each other. I also have three children that I left in my country and we were abandoned by their father. So we [Gemma and her employer] were like a support for each other."

Some of the leaders also have organizational experiences in their countries of origin and in Lebanon. Gemma, for instance, was the chairperson of a youth organization in her home town and was active in the student council in her school. At university she was also the president of the student council for a year. When she came to Lebanon she started volunteering in the activities and events of the Philippines embassy. In 2004 she became the chairperson of the Philippines Basketball League. In 2010 she left the league and started volunteering at different NGOs on issues of migrant domestic workers, attending workshops and seminars. As someone who is immersed in Filipina community organizing, she was approached by the ILO about the PAR, became active in the union, and became a member of its executive board. Gemma's personal trajectory, along with the relations she forged with her embassy and her access to NGOs, allowed her to gain prominence within her community and later in the union.

Besides the 'historical' community leaders such as Gemma, the union has facilitated the emergence of new leaders. Reflecting on this issue, Nabil, from the ILO, says:

> *Sri Lankans constitute the largest membership of the union together with Filipinas. These are historical [migrant worker] communities in Lebanon and their leadership is crucial in the mobilizing efforts. They are very active and have the respect of their community members. In comparison, the Malagasy community, for example, does not have historical community leaders. The current leaders were formed during the unionizing process, not before.* (Personal interview with Nabil, ILO staff and consultant for the trade union, February 2015)

In an unpublished report about the PAR, Carole Kerbage (2014) notes that despite the fact that dealing with community leaders has practical advantages, it might also lead to monopoly of power, and it is here that a paradox lies. Kerbage cautions that dealing with community leaders as spokespersons on behalf of their respective communities deepens the gap between the leaders and the other workers. She quoted one community leader saying: "Many women workers broke the barrier of fear and shame, but there is a significant disparity in experiences between us [the leaders] and the rest of the workers." This gap became apparent to Kerbage when she was interviewing one of the workers who took part in the PAR: "In response to my questions, the worker told me to address the questions to her leader, saying that the latter knows better than her" (Kerbage 2014).

It is clear that those who are endowed with relatively more social resources (such as education, connections, freedom of mobility) achieve the functions of leadership. The exercise of leadership rests broadly on this logic, by which the most socially privileged members have access to representation functions. These community leaders, however, are also recognized as having played a central role in the establishment of the union. As key persons with access to their migrant communities, they were the ones who propagated the news about the union and recruited new members.

Challenging State Power

For years, migrant workers, including domestic workers, had organized around communal lines, which aimed at promoting the community, strengthening and supporting its members, and mobilizing a cultural, religious, and national ethos. This community organizing aimed at retaining and cultivating the migrant communities' cultures and acted as support networks for domestic workers, especially those who suffered poor working conditions. In many of my interlocutors' personal narratives, there were stories of runaway domestic workers who sought support and assistance as they escaped their dire situations. Some of the members would host them temporarily at their homes, help them find another job, and approach a new *kafil*. In cases where runaway domestic workers were detained by the General Security, their fellow community members would collect money from each other to buy them an airplane ticket back home. Rose, for example, first came to Lebanon in 1999. Back then, a small community of Cameroonians was holding its monthly Sunday meetings in a small church in Dekweneh. One day, she met a Cameroonian domestic worker who told her about the community meetings. She started attending these meetings and eventually became the community leader. She recalls:

We mainly spoke about our problems at work. We complained and shared what was happening with us during the month. It was a way for us to evade and temporarily escape our work. When the Sunday meeting came, I was very happy. On Saturday night I prepared the shoes and the clothes that I was going to wear the next day. I would put them next to me on the bed. I waited for the alarm clock to ring so I could wake up and go meet my friends. I awaited this day, every month. It was very important for me. (Personal interview with Rose, union executive board member from Cameron, February 2015)

As Rose's narrative shows, these community meetings provided migrant women with the opportunity to gather and discuss important events in their lives. The stress she puts on the act of talking ("we spoke," "complained," "shared") suggests that these meetings created important communication networks among them.

The Lebanese state rarely perceived these migrant agglomerations as threatening; it rarely tried to break them, as they did not constitute themselves as openly contestational, challenging discriminatory policies affecting the migrant workers. I do not mean to suggest that they were apolitical spaces. On the contrary, they were politicized in the sense that they sought to forge solidarity among community members. Solidarity is indeed a political act, but one that does not necessarily aim to challenge the state, but rather to forge new modes of sociality and social interactions and being in a community. These community spaces were the first instances of politicization for many migrant domestic workers, such as Rose, who became a community leader and later a union militant. These communities created new avenues of access and mobilization and definitely provided the ground for new political subjects to emerge.

However, when the workers' organization took a turn toward open political resistance, in the form of a trade union for domestic workers, the government, through its Ministry of Labor, was quick to declare this form of organizing illegal, threatened to use security forces to break up their congress in 2015, and refused to grant their trade union a license.

In fact, on the eve of the launch of the trade union for domestic workers on January 25, 2015 ILO officials were threatened by the minister of labor, Sejaan Azzi. In a phone call, he declared their action an infringement of Lebanon sovereignty and in violation of its laws, as one ILO official told me. The minister also threatened to send the police to prevent the trade-union congress. However, FENASOL's leadership insisted on holding the conference despite the threats, benefiting from the presence and the support of the International Labour Organization, the International Trade Union Confederation, the International Federation of Domestic Workers, and the Arab Labor Organization, besides local support from various human-rights NGOs. The presence of the delegates from these organizations constituted a protection of the migrant domestic workers and ultimately curbed the minister's intention to forcefully break up the congress, which otherwise could have caused an international stir. The minister of labor, to fight the union, armed himself with the Labor Law, which explicitly excludes domestic workers from its protection and denies migrant workers the right to establish a trade union. However, in order to be consistent with the law limiting the establishing of the union to Lebanese citizens, the union for domestic workers was established as a committee under the General Union of Cleaning Workers and Social Care, and included Lebanese citizens who could submit a formal request to the Ministry of Labor for authorization.

Nor was it a coincidence that the workers' congress was attended by the representative of the Lebanese General Security (al-Amn al-'Aam al-Lubnani). The presence of the latter, along with the absence of a representative from the Ministry of Labor, was a reminder to the trade unionists that the only government office that deals with migrant workers in Lebanon is the General Security. Any initiative that concerns migrants should take place, if at all, under the direct auspices of the General Security—or the state's "hand that strikes," to borrow Agier and Fernbach's (2011) term. This statement was also a reminder of the exceptional status of migrant workers in the country, who are differently positioned from the national citizen in relation to the state. The state's management of migrant workers' lives through the General Security instead of the Ministry of Labor, for example, constructs the boundary between the migrant and the citizen. Their ineligibility for citizenship, which Yuval-Davis defines as "full membership in the community" (Yuval-Davis 1997: 59), their lack of social and political rights, and their exclusion from laws that govern national workers underline their status as temporary migrants, in a permanent state of exception. Within this context, FENASOL's organizing efforts with migrant domestic workers should be seen as a defiance of these exclusionary policies and racist discourses on migration and as a struggle against discrimination in the labor market based on gendered and racial lines. But to what extent is the Federation immune to the nationalistic discourse and ideology?

FENASOL's Ambivalent Politics toward Migrants

Despite the fact that FENASOL took the initiative to organize migrant domestic workers, and although the Federation undertook a revision of its bylaws and internal structures to make it inclusive of migrant workers (since it was previously exclusive to Lebanese workers), allowing them the same rights as Lebanese, FENASOL's politics and discourse on migrants remain ambivalent. The revisions that the Federation undertook, discussed, and voted on in its general assembly in 2015 gave the migrants the right to join the Federation's unions, to run for elections on the level of the federation representative boards, and to vote. These internal reforms, however, are contrary to FENASOL's public discourse, expressed in its published statements, which considers the migrant worker as an illegitimate competitor of the Lebanese worker. FENASOL's leadership rejects accusations that its discourse stirs nationalistic feelings, and it considers itself involved in struggles for the workers' rights irrespective of their nationalities, but it opposes the employers' quest to employ illegal and poorly paid migrants, which constitutes the basis of this 'illegitimate competition' in the labor market. Nevertheless, FENASOL's public statements take a stand against illegal migration rather than denouncing exploitation by employers. For instance, between 2014 and 2015, I collected dozens of statements issued by the Federation's affiliated unions, many of which call on the Ministry of Labor to intervene to put an end to the illegitimate competition between migrants and Lebanese and to stop the flow of illegal migration to the country, which was most easily done, in the case of Arab migrants, through Syria before 2011. For instance, on December 22, 2014, the executive board of the Bakeries Workers' Union in Beirut and Mount Lebanon (which is affiliated with FENASOL) issued the following statement:

> *The board found that the social and economic situation in the country is hurting workers in bakeries, who suffer from the competition of*

foreign workers and the displaced [Syrian] workers that started to
constitute a burden on all labor categories. Therefore, we call upon the
Ministry of Labor and all concerned to put an end to the abuses and
protect the Lebanese work force.

The use of words such as 'illegitimate competitors' undermines any notion of solidarity. Migrant workers are scapegoated for low labor standards and economic hardship. For example, a common statement issued by the Union of Employees in Hotels, Restaurants, and Cafés in the Lebanese Republic and the Union of the Lebanese Chefs on January 26, 2015, declared that the deterioration of the tourism sector is largely due to the replacement of qualified Lebanese workers by low-skilled migrant workers.

FENASOL's initiative to organize migrants in domestic work and its ongoing nationalistic discourse are contradictory in the sense that the Federation claims to be opposed to racism, but its statements remain anchored in nationalist discourse. This perhaps partly explains why the Federation has not been part of any visible campaigns against racist attacks on migrant workers, in particular against Syrian workers (Lebanese Labor Watch 2012). Some labor activists I met argue that FENASOL is only concerned about defending the rights of Lebanese workers, which contradicts the Federation's so-called communist principles of international solidarity. The question remains, however: why would FENASOL organize migrants in domestic work, if it still perceived migrant workers as a threat or competition?

One explanation could be that migrants in domestic work do not really constitute 'competition' for local domestic workers. The migrants in this sector outnumber the Lebanese, who do not perceive domestic work as an attractive job for many reasons, one being "social shame" (Fernandez and de Regt 2014:8) and another that it is poorly valued and remunerated. Another explanation could be that migrant domestic workers have become part of a global humanitarian agenda and many international donor organizations are providing funds for local initiatives seeking to help improve their working conditions. Organizing migrants in domestic work thus allows FENASOL to forge relations with international donor organizations and obtain access to funds. For instance, the project to unionize domestic workers was funded by the

ILO with an approximate amount of USD 61,500. The total amount was announced during the trade-union congress for domestic workers in order to maintain transparency with the workers. The announcement was coupled with an explanation of how and when the money was spent.

Despite its initiative to organize migrants in domestic work, FENASOL and its affiliated trade unions have not yet had a strategic discussion on how to organize migrant workers. The organizing of precarious workers, including migrants and other informal workers, continues not to be taken seriously. The specific instance of organizing migrant domestic workers appears as isolated in the absence of a conscious strategy for recruiting and organizing migrants and informal workers. This situation leads to an 'us versus them' class consciousness, tied to persistent nationalism.

The Politics of Feelings: Shame, Pride, and Pity

Contrary to popular perceptions, the union for domestic workers is not intended only for migrants. The union does not specify the nationality of its members. It is open to Lebanese nationals as well as to migrant women and men in domestic work. However, since the beginning of the unionization process, the organizers have seemed to focus solely on migrants of African and Asian origins. The PAR was implemented with migrant domestic workers and was designed to address the plight of the migrant domestic workers only. The working conditions of the Lebanese, Syrian, and Palestinian domestic workers remain unknown. Workers from these places continue to be far from the reach of the union and are not considered as a 'target group' for recruitment and outreach, which explains why the migrants are the largest constituency of the union membership. There is no doubt that organizing migrant domestic workers is an easier endeavor, since they have already established community networks, as discussed above, and there are particular locations and areas where they live, work, congregate, and meet on their days off (churches, markets, community centers, NGO activities). Similar community networks for local domestic workers do not exist, so that approaching them would not be as easy as in the case of migrant women. The growing association of paid domestic work with women of Asian and African origins has pushed Lebanese women to prefer to work as waitresses or cleaners in offices rather than working in houses, leading to a rigid racial division of gendered labor.

Lebanese, Syrians, and Palestinians continue to be employed as domestic workers, even though they are outnumbered by migrant women. However, the social shame attached to working in other people's homes, which is typical of local domestic workers, stands in opposition to the feeling of pride that the migrant unionists attach to their work. This pride and the resulting claim for recognition of domestic labor as work, upheld by the migrant domestic workers, act as a political motive for their recruitment. Conscious union strategy to approach local domestic workers could transform their moral economy of shame into politics of pride. Such a strategy would alter the definitions of, and the social responses to, the stigmatized attributes associated with paid domestic work as a source of shame, in the same way that many other social movements build and use emotional capital to mobilize and propel participants into collective action, which in its turn generates pride and solidarity.

The lack of connections made by the union between migrant and local domestic workers also has repercussions on the way the handful of Lebanese unionists discursively produce themselves and other migrants. In fact, three Lebanese women (one works as a house cook, the other as an office cleaner, and the third in accounting at a private company) were pushed by FENASOL's leadership to join the union for domestic workers and ultimately made their way to its executive board, which is made up of 12 women overall. The professions of these workers did not matter for the organizers. What mattered was their nationality. The union needed to have Lebanese membership in order to obtain a license from the Ministry of Labor. Hence the Lebanese, who submitted their papers to the ministry in order to get the license, became the legal 'safeguard' of the union and of its members before the state.

Maryam, a 36-year-old Lebanese accounting worker, was elected by the union's general assembly as its president. Maryam had no previous experience in union activities. She joined FENASOL in 2014 through its national campaign on the right to housing. At the request of Castro Abdallah, she joined the union for domestic workers and became its president in 2015. Maryam describes the role of the union that she leads.

I encourage the idea of a union for domestic workers so they stop being enslaved. I feel pity for them. Now they have a union so they know that they [the migrant women] are like us. They have the same rights similar to us who work in private companies. At my family house we employ a domestic worker from Bangladesh. I am always eager to share with her what I do and what we do in the union for them. She likes it and she even told her family in Bangladesh about it. I want the union to achieve the demands raised by the domestic workers—to gain something for them, so that when they come to work they won't be afraid of their employers and the placement agencies. We want to convey to them the idea that we, as Lebanese, stand by their side and we will gain for them their rights, but they have to be good to us as well. I previously worked in a maids' recruitment agency and I was bothered by the way the owner used to deal with them. (Personal interview with Maryam, president of the union for domestic workers, February 2015)

In my interview with Maryam, I felt unease with the language that she used, in particular the way in which she relates to the migrant domestic workers who form her constituency. Her choice of language can be considered not 'politically correct,' especially since it emanates from a union president who ideally should be grounded in the language of solidarity, resistance, and defiance, not the language of pity. However, her discourse reflects the way she positions herself in relation to migrant domestic workers. Maryam relates to the experience of domestic workers from her relatively more privileged position as a worker who is formally employed in a private company on a contract basis, which guarantees a minimum wage and social and health security, a minimum of rights that the migrants do not enjoy. Maryam is also speaking from her social position as a Lebanese national and as an employer of a migrant domestic worker, which has impact on the claims she makes. In speaking on behalf of the migrants, a line of demarcation is drawn between 'us' (the Lebanese) and 'them' (the migrants). By positioning herself as an outsider in relation to the domestic workers, as a Lebanese whose only purpose in the union is to save them, she dissociates herself from paid domestic work as a shameful activity. The problematic of this differentiation, other than the fact that it reproduces the hegemonic discourse on migration, is that it constructs the migrant worker as substantially different from the Lebanese. The issue of the shared labor experiences of Lebanese domestic workers and migrants is replaced with the discourse on how the native Lebanese are here to save the others.

It is helpful to dig deeper into the language of pity. Aradau (2004) argues that what she terms "politics of pity" can in some cases create commonalities and challenge the existing social order, which has caused suffering. In this framework, pity functions as "an anti-governmental technology, concerned with emancipation from particular systems of power" (Aradau 2004:257)—in this case, the power that regulates and governs migrant domestic workers and denies them their rights. However, Aradau cautions that pity and other emotions are socially constructed and shaped by social institutions and power relations. This is obvious in the way Maryam conditions sympathy toward migrants in return for "them being good to us," that is, doing what they are told to do.

Furthermore, there is a limit to Maryam's solidarity. Solidarity expresses an understanding that one's own interests and those of the other members of the same political community are aligned insofar as one inhabits shared political spaces with them, and it does involve a feeling of identification with others. However, being an employer of a domestic worker herself, Maryam's political solidarity cannot transgress the language of pity. In this context, her feeling of pity does not act as a base for "emancipation from systems of power"; rather, it is rooted in the power relations that structure her encounter with the Bangladeshi domestic worker she employs. Hence, the position she occupies as a union leader for domestic workers is very much conflated with her position as an employer of a domestic worker. Yet, by focusing on Maryam's discourse, I do not mean to imply that the discursive practices pertain to individual choices. The problem is a social one. As Alcoff (1991) argues, discursive practices are socially constructed and cannot be analyzed as simply the result of autonomous individual choices. In fact, "politics of pity" based on victimization has been advocated and practiced by various NGOs, including women's-rights NGOs (see chapter 3). They are part and parcel of the local and global human-rights regime on migration.

Finally, having a Lebanese woman presiding over a union for workers who are predominantly migrants displays a dual act of power. On one level, the state, by its laws and regulations, does not allow militant migrants to exercise their militancy to its full potential. The state's authority is always there to impose itself from the outside. The workers have to subordinate their position in the union to a formal Lebanese leadership that does not share their knowledge, their political history in organizing, or their working conditions as domestic workers. Still, for FENASOL, this strategy was the only option to engage the state's regulatory regime, which denies migrant domestic workers the right to form unions of their own. It was a tactic employed to withstand the government's rejection of the union and ultimately protect the migrant members from any potential arbitrary actions on the part of the state. This tactic shows the ways in which labor unions have entered the dynamic of the 'system' and became absorbed by the logic of regulation, where respect for the law takes precedence over labor agitation.

Redistribution Isn't Enough

FENASOL's involvement in the organizing of domestic workers involves the navigation of two distinct sets of issues. One converges with standard trade-union concerns, such as collective bargaining to ensure the domestic workers' rights to a day off, formal recognition of domestic work under the labor law, minimum wage, and ending the *kafala* system, which fall under what Fraser (1995) calls claims for "redistribution." In other words, these are concerns that emanate from the socioeconomic injustices that the migrant domestic worker faces. These claims were raised by the workers during their congress and were also commonly underlined by my interlocutors. Thus, the right to mobility and decent working conditions were the concerns raised by the workers irrespective of their nationalities. The other set of issues that FENASOL leadership finds difficult to handle are the gender-specific constraints and problems that women workers have to contend with in their daily lives, such as sexual violence. These issues continue to be perceived by the leadership of the Federation as not being part of its domain of intervention, but rather as the domain of expertise of the women's-rights groups. This is why the leadership expresses unease at having to deal with cases of rape and sexual harassment. Moreover, the leadership believes that the women who come to them to complain of sexual violence are being sent by NGOs in order to 'test' the Federation's commitment to domestic workers.

With the sudden increase in the membership of women domestic workers, FENASOL's leadership has had to contend with frequent cases of sexual abuse. However, the lack of knowledge and absence of internal mechanisms to deal with such issues remains a challenge. Under the current structure of the Federation, there are no gender-sensitive bodies through which women can seek support. Abdallah told me how he personally dealt with the case of one domestic worker who came to him asking for help when she was raped by her employer.

Two hours ago a Bangladeshi worker came to me. She also came four months earlier. Her employer raped her. She had the courage to tell me about the issue. She came back today. I told her, "You should file a legal case against him." But she's scared to face him.

He goes on to tell me about another case:

A few months back, a domestic worker who speaks French came to me. Rabie (an ILO staff) happened to be here, so he translated to me what she was saying. She was collapsing. I talked to her and I tried to encourage her to speak: "What was he [the employer] doing to you? Did he grab your hand?" She wasn't resisting him much. She was weaker at nights when he approaches her. She became uncomfortable when he started to use her mouth. I told her, "I don't care, we should file a legal complaint and the Federation will pay for it." I asked her if there were any evidence that she was raped. She replied that the last time he raped her was a week ago. She told me that she couldn't forget it. She cannot sleep or stop blaming herself. She used to accept having sex with him, but when the sex became oral, I think she didn't want it any more. And there are many similar cases, but the women refuse to file a legal complaint. (Personal interview with Castro Abdallah, president of FENASOL, February 2015)

Abdallah's accounts reveal many problems. First, the worker who comes to complain about sexual violence has no one to address but a man who clearly states that such cases are not his concern as a unionist. Meanwhile, the executive board of the newly born union for domestic workers does not yet have the capabilities to deal with individual cases. Second, the woman is not directly believed; her resistance to rape is questioned and she is asked if she can prove that she was raped. Third, the context in which she is offered a place to speak about her experience does not respect her profound need for anonymity and privacy ("Rabie happened to be there to translate"). We do not know whether the woman was comfortable with having another male stranger translating such a personal experience. Fourth, the woman is left with only one option: to file a legal complaint. This is the only support that the Federation could offer. Fifth, Abdallah expresses his surprise that the women refused to file a legal complaint; in so doing, he not only ignored women's understanding of their sexual vulnerability, but also minimized the particular dangers confronting women who publicly resist sexual exploitation. This denotes a complete ignorance of the profound impact of institutionalized (police and law) racism, sexism, and classism regarding women in general and women migrant workers in particular, and the privileged position that the alleged rapist, as a Lebanese male employer, has over his domestic worker.

A study conducted by the ILO and the Caritas Lebanon Migrant Center in 2014 found that migrant domestic workers' access to justice is very difficult. First, women are reluctant to file a case against their employers, as they know it is very difficult to change employers without their consent because of the *kafala*. Second, the report identifies structural loopholes in the legal system, which "discourages domestic workers by placing them in the position of defendants, even when they are victims of serious violations of the Penal and Civil Codes" (CLMC and ILO 2014). For instance, if the domestic worker leaves the residence of her employer without the latter's consent she is charged for violating the decree on the entry and stay of foreign nationals in Lebanon. The study also points to the "marginalization imposed by various actors, and in particular by the judiciary, on low-skilled foreigners" (CLMC and ILO 2014). For example, in certain cases involving migrant domestic workers, the report sent to the Public Prosecutor's Office made reference to offenses such as damage or injuries, but the prosecutor did not initiate legal proceedings against the alleged offender.

This situation shows how racial and class discrimination and male domination operate in a legally and culturally authorized system of exclusion for migrant and women workers. Hence, labor unions need to combine politics of redistribution and anti-racist/sexist politics, which are intertwined and cannot be separated, and which form a main constituent of the life of migrant domestic workers. For the workers, the concern is as much about social justice and redistribution as it is about gender justice and dignity. In that sense, the Federation cannot choose to deal with one aspect of their work and neglect the other aspect, as they both constitute the labor experience of women workers. Otherwise, the latter will be rendered victims twice: first by those who exploit their labor and then by those who claim to defend them.

Daughters or Coworkers?

I was at FENASOL one Sunday morning to interview Abdallah. Interviewing the president was my legitimate excuse to justify my presence at the Federation. Since my frequent requests failed to convince Abdallah to allow me to attend the domestic workers' meetings, I had to resort to this trick in order to get an ethnographic sense of the various activities and interactions at play within the Federation. I understood his rejection as largely due to the fact that he was afraid that an outsider's presence might jeopardize the newly born union, which was already under attack by the Ministry of Labor. He told me, for instance, how a local newspaper published an article disclosing the fact that the unionists had submitted their papers to request the union license from the ministry, something only a handful of people knew about. Such incidents made him suspicious about an 'alien' presence. His fear was also mediated by his sense that "the NGO people don't want FENASOL to succeed in its organizing endeavor: when the workers succeed to have their union, these people might find themselves jobless," as he said. He was also afraid that I might be sharing the 'union's secrets' with 'these people.' My assurances that my presence was exclusively related to my academic research and had nothing to do with tensions between the NGOs and FENASOL did not succeed in appeasing him. Despite his anxiety about my presence, Abdallah did not hesitate to tell me about the hidden distrust between the Federation's leadership and some of the NGOs. In other words, he trusted me enough to tell me about these usually unspoken tensions. However, the fact that I needed Abdallah's permission to attend the domestic workers' meetings, and not the permission of the domestic workers' unionists themselves, who should in principle enjoy sovereignty over their meetings, said a great deal about the relations of power between the domestic workers' unionists and the Federation's leadership. Furthermore, it was interesting for me to see how power is produced discursively by the different union actors.

On the day of the trade-union congress, a small ceremony took place following the formal proceedings, in which the active supporters of the union for domestic workers were handed symbolic gifts by the women militants. When Abdallah's turn came to receive his gift, dozens of union members started to cheer him by calling him "Papa," followed by a long round of applause. After witnessing this scene, I became more attuned to the language used by the union leadership and the workers in addressing each other. For example, Abdallah would often call the women *al-banat* (plural of *bint*), which in Arabic means 'girls' but can also mean 'daughters.' My Cameroonian interlocutor justified this by saying:

> *We always address Abdallah as "Papa," because it shows respect, and for us, respect is obligatory. . . . I cannot allow myself to be at the same level as him. He is the president of the Federation. In my head I think: He is the founder. But I am also not inferior to him. We are all comrades. I am not . . . how to explain? I respect . . . I have respect for him.* (Personal interview, February 2015)

It is common in Lebanon to hear employers talk about their domestic workers as 'daughters.' The worker, on her part, is usually expected to address her employers as 'Papa' and 'Mama.' This myth of close kinship is part of the effort to secure the worker's dependence and devotion to the family that employs her. In other words, this discursive intimacy usually entails granting the employer more control over the worker as guardian and protector. Inherent in this relation with the employers is that the domestic worker is not perceived as an independent woman. The 'daughter,' in this instance, is a person over whom moral and paternalistic power is exercised, and who is consequently expected to negate her own needs as an adult woman.

In the context of the union, however, the words *banat* and 'Papa' point to the conflicting position the domestic workers occupy as unionists and as domestic workers, a position that includes two contested elements: being unionists, which entails a status of parity and camaraderie with fellow unionists; and being a woman employed in domestic service, which pushes their supposed 'fellow unionists' to mobilize a discourse of protection and guardianship by calling them *banat*. This shows that the nature of the work, its location, and its gender are all contingent on the ways in which the workers are discursively produced within the labor union context. It also shows that the Federation, as an institution, is not immune to the discourse of guardianship that claims protection over the domestic worker in the family sphere. On the contrary, by reproducing the same discourse, a hierarchal relation is being forged between the women workers and the Federation leadership, following the image of Papa Abdallah and his *banat*. Hence, the mechanisms of domination, which structure social spaces and against which domestic workers are specifically trying to fight, are reproduced within the Federation.

Conclusion

This chapter has sought to analyze the politics emanating from the different union actors and non-governmental organizations I encountered during my fieldwork, and the power imbalances that shape the relations between them. I have discussed the ways in which solidarity is forged among women domestic workers across nationality lines, how class interests are expressed among them, and how, from these efforts, militant women leaders are emerging. In their action to form their union, the workers are challenging the state regulatory power that continuously produces them as 'exception' and 'excess' and denies them the right to organize, and thus to have a political voice. In that sense, their labor-rights activism implicitly critiques the exclusionary practices of citizenship by which access to rights is mediated. However, they have to navigate the minefield of power within the context of their union and the Federation's structure itself. For instance, we have seen the ways in which agitational politics is hindered by global governance, by reliance on external funding, and by the Federation's unwillingness to challenge the state regulatory regime. We have also seen the challenges in solidarity building where gender, class, and nationality limit the fragile alliances within the core group (such as in the case of the Lebanese leadership of the union for domestic workers); despite the best intentions of the FENASOL leadership, the masculinist ideology bounds the potentialities that can emanate from the union.

In fact, in the current economic climate and for the labor movement to ensure its relevance, there is no other option but to engage with the changing face of the labor force, which is increasingly migrant and feminized. This means that, besides organizing domestic workers, labor unions should develop strategies to organize the informal Lebanese and migrant workers. The labor unions must also address and defend the specific needs and rights of women workers, as well as their concerns as migrant workers, and the leadership role of women is limited under the Federation's current male-dominated bureaucracy. Despite the fact that the Federation has offered a space for domestic workers, to organize them is to grasp the different ways in which they are being exploited, not only as workers, but also as women and as migrants. Thus, the demands of women domestic workers for labor rights which are rooted in gendered and racialized analysis of work continue to pose conceptual challenges for the labor unions and for the women's-rights organizations. These issues need to be addressed in order to build a movement that does not merely seek to defend previously gained rights, but that acts to deeply transform the relations of exploitation under capitalism. In this struggle, the complex hierarchies and inequalities in power relations, including gender and race within social movements, have to be simultaneously addressed and transformed.

CHAPTER 5

The Prospects for Organizing Migrants in a National Framework

More than a Broom

I sat in a restaurant with Rose, a domestic worker from Cameroon and a member of the executive board of the union for domestic workers, on a Sunday afternoon, while she narrated her experience of working in Lebanon. The restaurant was empty except for an old couple sitting three tables away from us, which gave her space to speak freely. With an exasperated sigh she said, "You know? What we lack in our work is respect. The work we do is considered worthless." Her tone of voice changed and became louder as she continued:

> But no! It's not. Why is it that work you do with all of your sweat, your body, your heart, and your soul is considered worthless? No, this should not be so. You wake up in the morning at 6 am, you begin by preparing breakfast, you clean everything, then you pass to other things. You wash, you iron, then you have to run to pick up the children from the school bus, you give them something to eat, you clean up after them, then in the evening you prepare dinner and you clean again. You are the last one to sleep and the first one to wake up in the house. How can that be nothing? It should be honorable, because this is what it is. But today, in this society, people only see the broom. They don't see that behind the broomstick there's a human being who is pushing it. How can this not be considered work? If you consider that to be nothing, then send me back to my country and you do the 'nothingness' of the work that we do!

In tracing the work histories of migrant domestic workers, I often asked them: if they had the opportunity, what would they change about their conditions in Lebanon? Their answers varied, but one thing that appeared repeatedly in these narratives was the desire to enjoy a dignified existence. Their narratives were filled with stories about having to endure alienation from the social as racialized bodies, and ill-treatment from the society at large, from the taxi driver, to the cashier and customers in the supermarket, to the waiters at restaurants, and always from the police. Similarly, Rose's narration of her work experience centered on recognition. She did not complain about the workload or an overbearing employer as much as she deplored the misrecognition of her labor as "worthless," about people's appreciation of the broom more than the human being behind it. For someone whose job is the hard work of caring for others, the misrecognition of her labor struck her as absurd.

The metaphor of the broom recalls Marx's analysis of the worker's alienation from production, the self, and the other. It also serves to frame pressing questions about the undervaluation of caring labor, whether waged or unwaged, in relation to the legacy of their gendering and racialization. Domestic workers constitute an emblematic example of the ways in which workers' subjectivities are subsumed and merged with their labor under the new economy. The work they do is not about producing material things that are touched, but about things that are felt and sensed, that pertain to affect and care. In that regard, the 'broom' becomes an extension of the physical body of the worker and affect is produced through the constant interaction among the different bodies within the household. Since labor is embodied, Rose's expression of frustration is not only about the amount of labor she has to perform as much as it is about the fact that the misrecognition of her labor constitutes misrecognition of her humanness in itself.

Thus, I suggest that we read the workers' enthusiasm about their union, and the sense of pride emanating from their new collectivity, in relation to the desire that Rose expressed, that this labor be counted as worthy. Labor politics in that sense is tightly woven into the desire for recognition. For example, we might recall Gemma's description of how she encourages the union members to wave their union IDs. By doing this, she was not only gesturing to the importance of workers' collective identity, but also, and perhaps more importantly, soliciting in them dignity and pride, shedding the stigma of an activity associated in the wider social imaginary with shame and dirt.

The Nation and the Politics of Labor and Life

Recognition is also related to another desire that is usually unspoken and banned from the zone of formal labor politics, which is the desire for life. The recognition of the desire for life is part and parcel of the recognition of the workers as human beings. Migrant domestic workers are placed in the category of the migrant 'other' throughout their stay in Lebanon. They are perceived to be in the country for one thing—to push the broom. This is explicit, for example, in the ways in which employers deny their workers' sexuality, or, as Moukarbel puts it, "The maids are not permitted to exist as women in their own right, denied having friends and having a private life for the entire duration of their contract" (2009:329). In fact, migrant domestic workers are subject to a stringent discipline regarding their sexuality that is promoted by the state. For example, in 2015 the General Security issued a new directive, according to which an employer has to notify the General Security if the domestic worker gets involved "in any kind of relationships" or "gets married to a Lebanese or a foreigner residing in Lebanon." In such a case the worker is subject to deportation. In other words, the General Security directive declares that domestic workers are not allowed to love.

These kinds of policies governing migrant women workers that pertain to control, surveillance, and exclusion are usually not the subject of formal union policies, which are concerned with work disputes taking place at the work site between the employers and the workers. However, life includes all the other things that people do outside work. In that sense, domestic workers constitute a challenge to the labor unions, because their labor is embodied and their entire being is disciplined and instrumentalized. Their lives are not expected to know leisure, love, and sociality; they are entirely reduced to labor. Mala's example, presented earlier, speaks volumes regarding this issue. Mala, who lived and worked in Lebanon as a domestic worker for more than 30 years, is now obliged to retire to her 'home country,' Sri Lanka. Her narrative destabilizes our understanding of what constitutes 'home' and national belonging. The politics of life must include all aspects of life as it is lived here and now. Beyond laboring—as we all labor, whether sitting behind a desk or pushing a broom—it pertains to sociality, to the right to claim membership in the society in which one lives and works, to have a say in determining the conditions that affect everyday life, and to be able to transform the conditions of institutional subordination. This means that labor unions, if they are to be reinvented, will have to open up to fields outside of the production of physical goods.

I perceive the union for migrant domestic workers as an attempt that has the potentiality of destabilizing the exclusion that the logic of the nation-state, as protector of capital, imposes upon migrant workers, who are recognized solely as a source for constant inflow of low-wage labor (Parreáas 2001). The migrants become these bodies whose exclusion is essential in maintaining the space of the nation's sovereignty, which is imagined as coherent and homogeneous. Asking the question from the position of labor allows us to open up the imagination to other forms of sociality that transgress national distinctions. It also allows us to look at the ways in which workers, and migrant workers in particular, are continuously challenging the nation's order and orderliness, even while they remain the object of state and capital regulation (Walters 2002; Appadurai 2003). I argue in favor of a politics that gives the migrants the right to make choices in the country where they live, and I suggest that labor politics be used as a means to fight against the exclusion of migrant workers from life.

Organizing the Excluded

For more than four years I have been engaged as a militant, a journalist, and a researcher with most of the labor actions that have taken place in Lebanon. I have watched informal workers, migrants, and the Lebanese working class struggle in vain to achieve the most basic rights, such as a minimum wage and secure jobs. I have seen the ways in which these workers' actions have been easily crushed by an alliance between the government and the employers, and disregarded by the formal trade-union organizations. Since the 1990s the labor unions have moved through a steady path toward bureaucratic and service-oriented unions. Privileging a Fordist model of organizational structure, despite the fact that this model has become a historical artifact, labor unions have played an active role in further excluding the majority of workers. For example, chapter 2 shows that more than 90 percent of the enterprises in Lebanon employ fewer than ten workers, that migrant workers constitute a considerable portion of the work force, and that the majority of the work force (both migrant and Lebanese) is concentrated in the informal sector. The neoliberal onslaught has affected working conditions and livelihoods, and has rendered older forms of union organizing ineffective. The administrative structures of the main labor unions have largely become instruments of state regulatory actions. Unions, even those coming out of the Lebanese left, have turned into bureaucratic, male-dominated organizations, demobilized and manipulated by the authority at the same time as they have been effectively stripped of a broad political function.

Given these contemporary conditions, I approached the initiative to organize migrant domestic workers in a union, under the auspices of FENASOL, the ILO, and the NGOs, with skepticism, viewing these bodies as an organizing structure that is highly mitigated by relations of power between the different actors over gender and nationality lines, as well as a project that is driven by international governance. This fact leads us to pose the question of why international capital, at this particular moment, is interested in initiating and supporting labor-union organizing, and to what emancipatory goals. Have labor unions given up on agitational politics for short-term funded project initiatives?

Despite the fact that the union is in its preliminary stages and that there are limits to the generalizations that can be made from this experience, the actors' discourses, especially at the level of FENASOL's leadership, do not reflect a political commitment to building real alliances with migrant workers. Rather, FENASOL's initiative to organize migrant domestic workers can be best understood in relation to the opportunity that global governance (ILO) offers the Federation in terms of funding and visibility, with no need for a genuine commitment to build a strong and combative labor movement. On this level, one example is telling. On the occasion of May 1, International Workers' Day, when the newly formed union for domestic workers called for a protest demanding that the union be recognized by the Lebanese government, none of FENASOL's affiliated unions marched in solidarity with the domestic workers. This expresses the fact that organizing migrant domestic workers continues to be a contested project within

FENASOL, with Lebanese union leaders considering it a secondary project at a time when 'Lebanese' workers are unorganized. Thus, beyond the formal organizing of migrants (domestic workers), labor solidarity needs to be tested on the ground, in the practices and discourses of the Lebanese unionists.

At the same time, the women migrants are aware of the contradictions and limitations of their unionization and also of the actions of the NGOs on their behalf. They have on many occasions reacted to the discourses that victimize them, and claimed ownership of their union. Perhaps it is because of all these factors that the union gives hope, as it is at the very least offering possibilities of reworking ideas of labor organizing. If nothing else, the energies, enthusiasm, and hope consistently expressed by the migrant domestic workers are to be taken seriously. Bringing together migrant women from the global south, who have been driven by the devastating effects of capitalist globalization to migrate and work in private households under exploitative working conditions, in a job that is excluded and invisible, perceived as 'shameful' and 'dirty,' is a reminder that workers in even the most isolating employment can attempt to reconfigure the relations of power and inequality that underpin their working conditions. Redirecting the site of the struggle from narrowly defined workplace disputes to public contestations over the value and meaning of work is an important step for rethinking questions of labor organizing in the contemporary environment. Although these efforts may not directly subvert existing hierarchies and inequalities, they generate visibility for excluded workers, joining demands for redistribution with demands for recognition, as Fraser (1995) suggests.

Rather than question whether it is possible to organize more vulnerable segments of the work force, such as migrants and women, the unionization of migrant domestic workers obliges us to shift the debate to examine how and under what conditions the excluded can leverage any power at all. With millions of migrant workers in the Arab world, the question for those concerned with social change is how to benefit from the migrants' considerable presence and work on building their organized political power. How can strong alliances be built across nationality lines to enhance political change? And what effects might this have on our imagination of the political and the social?

Irrespective of whether the union members succeed in attaining the minimum rights they are struggling for, what is more important is that they are engaging in an attempt, learning through it, and teaching us at the same time to challenge the structural inequities and the values of sexism and racism that are part and parcel of our capitalist present. Their struggle, in my view, is not only about winning small gains; it is about opening up space for the excluded to have a say in determining the conditions of their existence. By virtue of this struggle they are transformed, and are transforming society with them. As Gemma puts it, "Having this union was one of those historical moments when everyone present knew that an important barrier had been crossed, that there would be no turning back."

Finally, in this research I have tried to situate the question of migrant domestic workers in relation to the labor movement on one level and to the women's-rights movement on another. The goal is to analyze the organizing of the domestic workers within its broader social context, highlighting the challenges and the possibilities residing in this attempt, rather than looking at migrant domestic workers as an isolated and exceptional labor category under neoliberalism. This research has also sought to grasp the fleeting moment of initiating the union, which contains a certain potentiality in spite of the threats that surround it and the contradictions within it. That potentiality is the intrusion of the excluded into the sociopolitical space, or what Zizek (2009) calls the "universality of the social body." In fact, throughout the writing of the thesis, Lenin's question, reiterated by Zizek, came continually to mind: "How to begin from the beginning?" In other words, how to imagine alternative movements that constantly promote inclusion and that act to destroy the contemporary forms of social apartheid that divide people along national, gender, racial, and sectarian lines.

But how can we expect the migrants to form strong political and labor movements while their mobility within the society that hosts them is almost nonexistent and where institutional sectarianism, coupled with social injustice, has succeeded in bringing the society to its knees? Could the impasse in which Lebanese society found itself—social movements and labor movements included—be overcome by the migrants, the very people who are the most excluded and marginalized in this society? Does not this presumption throw the burden of the 'failed revolution' and social inaction on those who are the most fragile and the most precarious?

There is no easy answer to these questions. I think that the brave act of the migrant domestic workers in asserting themselves and reclaiming labor and human rights that have been denied to them is a first step toward the inclusion of the excluded that has been discussed earlier, and it will have permanent effects on other 'aliens.' History has shown, in various contexts, that while social movements may have different agendas, they build on each other's histories, failures, and successes. The call for *isqat al-nizam* ('fall of the regime') in Tunisia and Egypt found its echoes in Greece, and the *midan* ('square') occupation in Egypt made its way as far as the US.

The migrant domestic workers in Lebanon, through their action, are forcing the attention of the nation to the fact that the migrant labor force has become a considerable part of society and can no longer be sidelined. From this point of view, it is no coincidence that on the eve of International Workers' Day, May 1, 2015, the only serious call for mobilization came from the migrant domestic workers in Lebanon claiming their union's right to be recognized. This fact is very telling, and in this very fact the whole story resides.

Bibliography

Abisaab, M. 2010. *Militant Women of a Fragile Nation*. Syracuse, NY: Syracuse University Press.

Agier, M., and D. Fernbach. 2011. *Managing the Undesirables: Refugee Camps and Humanitarian Government*. Cambridge, UK: Polity Press.

Alcoff, L. 1991. "The Problem of Speaking for Others," *Cultural Critique*, 20: 5–32.

Andrijasevic, R. 2007. "Beautiful Dead Bodies: Gender, Migration, and Representation in Anti-Trafficking Campaigns," *Feminist Review*, 86: 24–44.

Appadurai, A. 2003. "Sovereignty without Territoriality: Notes for a Postnational Geography." In P. Yaeger, ed. *The Geography of Identity*, 40–58. Ann Arbor: University of Michigan Press.

Aradau, C. 2004. "The Perverse Politics of Four-Letter Words: Risk and Pity in the Securitisation of Human Trafficking," *Millennium-Journal of International Studies*, 33(2): 251–277.

———. 2008. *Rethinking Trafficking in Women: Politics out of Security*. Basingstoke, UK: Palgrave Macmillan.

al-'Aris, M. 1982. *Mustafa al-'Aris yatadhakar*. Beirut: Dar al-Farabi.

Arnold, D., and Bongiovi, J. R. 2013. "Precarious, Informalizing, and Flexible Work: Transforming Concepts and Understandings," *American Behavioral Scientist*, 57(3): 289–308.

Badran, I., and M. Zbeeb. 2011. "Moqaraba naqdiya li-l wad' al-naqabi al-'ummali al-rahen." Unpublished article.

Baroudi, S. E. 1998. "Economic Conflict in Postwar Lebanon: State-Labor Relations between 1992 and 1997," *The Middle East Journal*, 52(4): 531–550.

Bou Habib, A. 2011. "Al-ba'd min tarikh al-haraka al-naqabiya." *Ittihad naqabat mouwazzafi al-masaref.* November 16. http://www.fsebl.com/CustomPage.aspx?Editor_ID=16

Bourdieu, P. 1998. "The Essence of Neoliberalism," *Le Monde Diplomatique*, December 8.

Brahic, B., et al. 2011. "L'organisation des travailleuses dans le secteur de l'exportation horticole: Études de cas d'Afrique de l'Est," *Travail, capital et société*, 44(1): 70–97.

Brown, W. 2000. "Suffering Rights as Paradoxes," *Constellations*, 7(2): 230–241.

———. 2006. *Regulating Aversion: Tolerance in the Age of Identity and Empire.* Princeton: Princeton University Press.

———. 2009. *Wounded Attachments.* London: Routledge.

Butler, J. 1993. *Bodies that Matter: On the Discursive Limits of 'Sex.'* New York: Routledge.

al-Buwari, I. 1986. *Tarikh al-haraka al-'ummaliya wa-l-naqabiya fi Lubanan: 1908–1946.* Beirut: Dar al-Farabi.

Chalcraft, J. 2009. *The Invisible Cage: Syrian Migrant Workers in Lebanon.* Stanford, CA: Stanford University Press.

Chang, D. 2009. "Informalising Labour in Asia's Global Factory," *Journal of Contemporary Asia*, 39(2): 161–179.

———. 2012. "The Neoliberal Rise of East Asia and Social Movements of Labour: Four Moments and a Challenge," *Interface*, 4(2): 22–51. http://www.interfacejournal.net/

Chit, B. 2014. "Sectarianism and the Arab Revolutions," *Socialist Review*, February. http://socialistreview.org.uk/388/sectarianism-and-arab-revolutions

CLMC and ILO. 2014. "Access to Justice for Migrant Domestic Workers in Lebanon." http://www.ilo.org/wcmsp5/groups/public/---arabstates/---ro-beirut/documents/genericdocument/wcms_247033.pdf

Cook, A. 1981. "The Most Difficult Revolution: Women and Trade Unions," *Equal Opportunities International*, 1(2): 9–11.

Cornwall, A. 2013. "Preface." In N. Kabeer, R. Sudardshan, and K. Milward, eds. *Organizing Women Workers in the Informal Economy: Beyond the Weapons of the Weak*, viii–xii. London: Zed Books.

Daou, B. 2014. "Les féminismes au Liban: Un dynamisme de position-nement par rapport au patriarcat et un renouvellement au sein du 'Printemps Arabe.'" Unpublished master's thesis: Université Saint-Joseph, Beirut.

Davidson, J. 2006. "Will the Real Sex Slave Please Stand Up?" *Feminist Review*, 83: 4–22.

de Regt, M. 2010. "Ways to Come, Ways to Leave: Gender, Mobil-ity, and Il/legality among Ethiopian Domestic Workers in Yemen," *Gender & Society*, 24(2): 237–260.

Doraï, M. K., and O. Clochard. 2006. "Non-Palestinian Refugees in Leb-anon: From Asylum Seekers to Illegal Migrants." In F. De Bel Air, ed. *Migration and Politics in the Middle East: Migration Policies, Nation Building and International Relations*, 127–143. Beirut: IFPO.

Engels, F. 1972. *The Origin of the Family, Private Property, and the State, in the Light of the Researches of Lewis H. Morgan*. New York: International.

Enslin, E. 1994. "Beyond Writing: Feminist Practice and Limitations of Ethnography," *Cultural Anthropology*, 9(4): 537–568.

Esim, S., and C. Kerbage. 2011. *The Situation of Migrant Domestic Work-ers in Arab States: A Legislative Overview*. Beirut: ESCWA.

Fernandez, B., and M. de Regt. 2014. *Migrant Domestic Workers in the Middle East: The Home and the World*. New York: Palgrave Macmillan.

Fillieule, O., L. Mathieu, and C. Péchu, eds. 2009. *Dictionnaire des mou-vements sociaux*. Paris: Presses de la Fondation nationale des sciences politiques.

Fraser, N. 1995. "From Redistribution to Recognition: Dilemmas of Justice in a Post-Socialist Age," *New Left Review*, 212: 68–93.

Graham, J. 2000. *Class and Its Others*. Minneapolis: University of Min-nesota Press.

Gutierrez-Rodríguez, E. 2007. "The 'Hidden Side' of the New Economy: On Transnational Migration, Domestic Work, and Unprecedented Intimacy," *Frontiers: A Journal of Women's Studies*, 28(3): 60–83.

———. 2010. *Migration, Domestic Work, and Affect: A Decolonial Approach on Value and the Feminization of Labor*. New York: Routledge.

Gutmann, M. 1993. "Rituals of Resistance: A Critique of the Theory of Everyday Forms of Resistance," *Latin American Perspectives*, 7(20): 74–92.

Hamdan, K. 2003. *Micro and Small Enterprises in Lebanon.* ERF Research Report RR0417. http://www.erf.org.eg/CMS/uploads/pdf/1183634799_RR0417.pdf

Hamill, K. 2011. *Trafficking of Migrant Domestic Workers in Lebanon: A Legal Analysis.* Kafa. http://www.kafa.org.lb/StudiesPublication-PDF/PRpdf37.pdf

Hardt, M. 1996. "Introduction: Laboratory Italy." In P. Virno and M. Hardt, eds. *Radical Thought in Italy: A Potential Politics*, 1–12. Minneapolis: University of Minnesota Press.

Harvey, D. 2005. *A Brief History of Neoliberalism.* Oxford: Oxford University Press.

Human Rights Watch. 2008. "Lebanon: Protect Domestic Workers from Abuse, Exploitation." April 30. http://www.hrw.org/news/2008/04/29/lebanon-protect-domestic-workers-abuse-exploitation

———. 2014. "Lebanon Migrant Workers' Children Expelled." September 3. http://www.hrw.org/news/2014/09/02/lebanon-migrant-workers-children-expelled

Jad, I. 2004. "The NGO-ization of Arab Women's Movements," *IDS Bulletin*, 35(4): 34–42.

Jureidini, R. 2009. "In the Shadows of Family Life: Toward a History of Domestic Service in Lebanon," *Journal of Middle East Women's Studies*, 5(3): 74–101.

———. 2011a. *Exploratory Study of Psychoanalytic and Social Factors in the Abuse of Migrant Domestic Workers by Female Employers in Lebanon.* Beirut: Kafa. http://www.kafa.org.lb/StudiesPublicationPDF/PRpdf38.pdf

———. 2011b. "State and Non-State Actors in Evacuations during the Conflict in Lebanon, July–August 2006." In K. Koser and S. Martin, eds. *The Migration–Displacement Nexus: Concepts, Cases and Responses*, 197–215. New York: Berghahn Books.

Jureidini, R., and N. Moukarbel. 2004. "Female Sri Lankan Domestic Workers in Lebanon: A Case of 'Contract Slavery'?" *Journal of Ethnic and Migration Studies*, 30(4): 581–607.

Kabeer, N., K. Milward, and R. Sudarshan. 2013. *Organizing Women Workers in the Informal Economy: Beyond the Weapons of the Weak.* London: Zed Books.

Kaedbey, D. 2015. "Shadow Feminism in Lebanon, Part One," *Sawt al-Niswa*. http://sawtalniswa.com/article/460

Kafa. 2013. "Launch of the Campaign 'We Have a Mission: If You're Threatened, Do Not Hesitate to Call 112.'" November, 25. http://www.kafa.org.lb/kafa-news/68/launch-of-the-campaign-we-have-a-mission-if-youre

————. 2014. "Dreams for Sale: The Exploitation of Domestic Workers from Recruitment in Nepal and Bangladesh to Working in Lebanon." http://www.kafa.org.lb/videos/29/dreams-for-sale-the-exploitation-of-domestic-worke

Kerbage, C. 2014. "The Participatory Research on Organizing Migrant Domestic Workers." Beirut: ILO, unpublished report.

Khalaf, M. 2002. "Women's Employment in Lebanon and Its Impact on Their Status." eScholarship. University of California. https://escholarship.org/uc/item/0611197h

Khater, F. 1996. "'House' to 'Goddess of the House': Gender, Class, and Silk in Nineteenth-Century Mount Lebanon," *International Journal of Middle East Studies*, 28(3): 325–348.

Lazzarato, M. 2009. "Neoliberalism in Action: Inequality, Insecurity, and the Reconstitution of the Social," *Theory, Culture & Society*, 26(6): 109–133.

Lebanese Labor Watch. 2012. "Waqe' al-'ummal al-souriyin 'am 2012: khatf, wa darb, wa salb, wa-l jounat 'majhouloun.'" http://daleel-madani.org/sites/default/files/BookletSyrianWorkers%20(2).pdf

————. 2013. "Al-Marsad ya'qod liqa' hiwari li-itlaq dirasatihi." October 24. http://lebaneselw.com/content/%D8%A7%D9%84%D9%85%D8%B1%D8%B5%D8%AF-%D9%8A%D8%B9%D9%82%D8%AF-%D9%84%D9%82%D8%A7%D8%A1%D8%A7-%D8%AD%D9%88%D8%A7%D8%B1%D9%8A%D8%A7-%D9%84-D8%A7%D8%B7%D9%84%D8%A7%D9%82-%D8%AF%D8%B1%D8%A7%D8%B3%D8%A7%D8%A7%D9%87-%D8%B9%D9%86-%D8%A7%D9%84%D9%85%D9%8A%D8%A7%D9%88%D9%85%D9%8A%D9%86-%D8%A8%D9%85%D8%B4%D8%A7%D8%B1%D9%83%D8%A9-%D8%B9%D9%85D8%A7%D9%84%D9%8A%D8%A9

Mahdavi, P. 2011. *Gridlock: Labor, Migration, and Human Trafficking in Dubai*. Stanford, CA: Stanford University Press.

Makarem, G., and A. Rizk. 2014. "Masculinities under Threat: Sexual Rights Organizations and the Masculinist State in Lebanon," *Civil Society Review*, 1: 97–108.

Manicom, L. 2001. "Globalising 'Gender' in, or as, Governance? Questioning the Terms of Local Translations," *Agenda*, 48: 6–21.

Millar, K. 2014. "The Precarious Present: Wageless Labor and Disrupted Life in Rio de Janeiro, Brazil," *Cultural Anthropology*, 29(1): 32–53.

Mitri, D. 2014. "From Public Space to Office Space: The Professionalization/NGO-ization of the Feminist Movement Associations in Lebanon and Its Impact on Mobilization and Achieving Social Change," *Civil Society Review*, 1: 87–98.

Moors, A., R. Jureidini, F. Ozbay, and R. Sabban. 2009. "Migrant Domestic Workers: A New Public Presence in the Middle East?" Social Science Research Council, 177–202. https://www.researchgate.net/profile/Ferhunde_Ozbay/publication/235936413_Publics_Politics_and_Participation_Locating_the_Public_Sphere_in_the_Middle_East_and_North_Africa/links/0fcfd5148193871c9e000000.pdf

Motaparthy, P. 2015. "Understanding Kafala: An Archaic Law at Cross-Purposes with Modern Development." Migrants-Rights.org. http://www.migrant-rights.org/2015/03/understanding-kafala-an-archaic-law-at-cross-purposes-with-modern-development/

Moukarbel, N. 2009. "Not Allowed to Love? Sri Lankan Maids in Lebanon," *Mobilities*, 4(3): 329–347.

Ng, C. 2004. "Women Workers in Malaysia (1980–2004) Part II: Emerging Issues—Migrant Workers and Sex Workers," *Aliran Monthly*. http://www.aliran.com/oldsite/monthly/2004a/5f.html

Ong, A. 2006. *Neoliberalism as Exception: Mutations in Citizenship and Sovereignty*. Durham, NC: Duke University Press.

Pande, A. 2012. "From 'Balcony Talk' and 'Practical Prayers' to Illegal Collectives: Migrant Domestic Workers and Meso-Level Resistances in Lebanon," *Gender & Society*, 26(3): 382–405.

Papadopoulos, D., and N. Stephenson. 2008. *Escape Routes: Control and Subversion in the Twenty-First Century*. London: Pluto Press.

Parreáas, R. 2001. "Transgressing the Nation-State: The Partial Citizenship and 'Imagined (Global) Community' of Migrant Filipina Domestic Workers," *Signs*, 26(4): 1129–1154.

Peteet, J. 1996. "From Refugees to Minority: Palestinians in Post-War Lebanon," *Middle East Report*, 200: 27–30.

Picard, E. 2013. "The Arab Uprisings and Social Rights: Asian Migrant Workers in Lebanon." IREMAM-CNRS Aix-en-Provence, France. https://hal.archives-ouvertes.fr/halshs-00938259/document

Salameh, R. 2014. "Gender Politics in Lebanon and the Limits of Legal Reformism." Civil Society Knowledge Center. September 16. http://cskc.daleel-madani.org/paper/gender-politics-lebanon-and-limits-legal-reformism

Sangster, J. 1994. "Telling Our Stories: Feminist Debates and the Use of Oral History," *Women's History Review*, 3(1): 5–28.

Scott, J. 1985. *Weapons of the Weak: Everyday Forms of Peasant Resistance.* New Haven: Yale University Press.

Shahnawaz, S. 2002. "Dual Labor Markets and Public Debt: An Illustration Using the Lebanese Example." http://www.luc.edu/orgs/meea/volume4/article.pdf

Stacey, J. 1988. "Can There Be a Feminist Ethnography?" *Women's Studies International Forum*, 11(1): 21–27.

Tabar, P. 2010. *Lebanon: A Country of Emigration and Immigration.* Beirut: LAU Press.

Tayah, M. 2012. *Working with Migrant Domestic Workers in Lebanon (1980–2012): A Mapping of NGO Services.* Beirut: ILO.

Traboulsi, F. 2014. *Social Classes and Political Power in Lebanon.* Beirut: Heinrich Böll Stiftung.

———. 2015. "Compassionate Communalism: Welfare and Sectarianism in Lebanon, for Melani Cammett." Issam Fares Institute for Policy and International Affairs, AUB, Beirut. Lecture, January 22.

Walters, W. 2002. "Deportation, Expulsion, and the International Police of Aliens," *Citizenship Studies*, 6(3): 265–292.

Wright, M. 2006. *Disposable Women and Other Myths of Global Capital.* New York: Routledge.

Yuval-Davis, N. 1997. *Gender and Nation.* London: Sage Publications.

Zizek, S. 2009. "How to Begin from the Beginning," *New Left Review*, May–June. http://newleftreview.org/II/57/slavoj-zizek-how-to-begin-from-the-beginning

About the Author

Farah Kobaissy is senior research assistant at the Asfari Institute for Civil Society and Citizenship at the American University of Beirut (AUB). This monograph is based on her MA thesis in gender and women's studies, the American University in Cairo. The thesis won the 25th January Award for Scholarly Excellence in 2015.

CAIRO PAPERS IN SOCIAL SCIENCE

Volume Six

1   *The Political Economy of Revolutionary Iran,* Mihssen Kadhim
2   *Urban Research Strategies in Egypt,* Richard A. Lobban, ed.
3   *Non-alignment in a Changing World,* Mohammed el-Sayed Selim, ed.
4   *The Nationalization of Arabic and Islamic Education in Egypt: Dar al-Alum and al-Azhar,* Lois A. Arioan

Volume Seven

1   *Social Security and the Family in Egypt,* Helmi Tadros
2   *Basic Needs, Inflation and the Poor of Egypt,* Myrette el-Sokkary
3   *The Impact of Development Assistance On Egypt,* Earl L. Sullivan, ed.
4   *Irrigation and Society in Rural Egypt,* Sohair Mehanna, Richard Huntington, and Rachad Antonius

Volume Eight

1,2   *Analytic Index of Survey Research in Egypt,* Madiha el-Safty, MontePalmer, and Mark Kennedy

Volume Nine

1   *Philosophy, Ethics and Virtuous Rule,* Charles E. Butterworth
2   *The 'Jihad': An Islamic Alternative in Egypt,* Nemat Guenena
3   *The Institutionalization of Palestinian Identity in Egypt,* Maha A. Dajani
4   *Social Identity and Class in a Cairo Neighborhood,* Nadia A. Taher

Volume Ten

1   *Al-Sanhuri and Islamic Law,* Enid Hill
2   *Gone For Good,* Ralph Sell
3   *The Changing Image of Women in Rural Egypt,* Mona Abaza
4   *Informal Communities in Cairo: the Basis of a Typology,* Linda Oldham, Haguer el Hadidi, and Hussein Tamaa

Volume Eleven

1   *Participation and Community in Egyptian New Lands: The Case of South Tahrir,* Nicholas Hopkins et al.
2   *Palestinian Universities Under Occupation,* Antony T. Sullivan
3   *Legislating Infitah: Investment, Foreign Trade and Currency Laws,* Khaled M. Fahmy
4   *Social History of An Agrarian Reform Community in Egypt,* Reem Saad

Volume Twelve

1 *Cairo's Leap Forward: People, Households, and Dwelling Space,* Fredric Shorter
2 *Women, Water, and Sanitation: Household Water Use in Two Egyptian Villages,* Samiha el-Katsha et al.
3 *Palestinian Labor in a Dependent Economy: Women Workers in the West Bank Clothing Industry,* Randa Siniora
4 *The Oil Question in Egyptian-Israeli Relations, 1967–1979: A Study in International Law and Resource Politics,* Karim Wissa

Volume Thirteen

1 *Squatter Markets in Cairo,* Helmi R. Tadros, Mohamed Feteeha, and Allen Hibbard
2 *The Sub-culture of Hashish Users in Egypt: A Descriptive Analytic Study,* Nashaat Hassan Hussein
3 *Social Background and Bureaucratic Behavior in Egypt,* Earl L. Sullivan, el Sayed Yassin, Ali Leila, and Monte Palmer
4 *Privatization: the Egyptian Debate,* Mostafa Kamel el-Sayyid

Volume Fourteen

1 *Perspectives on the Gulf Crisis,* Dan Tschirgi and Bassam Tibi
2 *Experience and Expression: Life Among Bedouin Women in South Sinai,* Deborah Wickering
3 *Impact of Temporary International Migration on Rural Egypt,* Atef Hanna Nada
4 *Informal Sector in Egypt,* Nicholas S. Hopkins ed.

Volume Fifteen

1 *Scenes of Schooling: Inside a Girls' School in Cairo,* Linda Herrera
2 *Urban Refugees: Ethiopians and Eritreans in Cairo,* Dereck Cooper
3 *Investors and Workers in the Western Desert of Egypt: An Exploratory Survey,* Naeim Sherbiny, Donald Cole, and Nadia Makary
4 *Environmental Challenges in Egypt and the World,* Nicholas S. Hopkins, ed.

Volume Sixteen

1 *The Socialist Labor Party: A Case Study of a Contemporary Egyptian Opposition Party,* Hanaa Fikry Singer
2 *The Empowerment of Women: Water and Sanitation Initiatives in Rural Egypt,* Samiha el Katsha and Susan Watts
3 *The Economics and Politics of Structural Adjustment in Egypt: Third Annual Symposium*

3   *Femininity and Dance in Egypt: Embodiment and Meaning in al-Raqs al-Baladi*, Noha Roushdy
4   *Negotiating Space: The Evolution of the Egyptian Street, 2000–2011*, Dimitris Soudias

Volume Thirty-three

1   *Masculinities in Egypt and the Arab World: Historical, Literary, and Social Science Perspectives*, Helen Rizzo, ed.
2   *Anthropology in Egypt 1900–1967: Culture, Function, and Reform*, Nicholas S. Hopkins
3   *The Church in the Square: Negotiations of Religion and Revolution at an Evangelical Church in Cairo*, Anna Jeannine Dowell
4   *The Political Economy of the New Egyptian Republic*, Nicholas S. Hopkins, ed.

Volume Thirty-four

1   *Egyptian Hip-Hop: Expressions From the Underground*, Ellen R. Weis
2   *Sports and Society in the Middle East*, Nicholas S. Hopkins and Sandrine Gamblin, eds.

Printed in the USA
CPSIA information can be obtained
at www.ICGtesting.com
JSHW012321031123
51441JS00004B/30